STAY CONNECTED TO CHRIST

BY DAVID AMOAH

LIFE AND SUCCESS PUBLISHING
www.abookinsideyou.com

Copyright 2020 © Pastor David Amoah

All rights reserved. No part of this publication may be produced, distributed, or transmitted in any form or by any means, including photocopying, recording, or other electronic or mechanical methods, without the prior written permision of the publisher, except in the case of brief quotations embodied in critical reviews and certain other noncommercial uses permitted by copyright law.

For permission requests, write to the publisher, addressed "Attention: Permissions Coordinator" at the email address below:

Life and Success Media Ltd

e-mail: info@abookinsideyou.com

www.abookinsideyou.com

Unless otherwise stated, all scripture quotations are taken from the Holy Bible, New King James Version. Quotations marked NKJV are taken from the HOLY BIBLE, NEW KING JAMES VERSION. Copyright © 1973, 1978, 1984 by International Bible Society. Used by permission of Hodder and Stoughton Ltd, a member of the Hodder Headline Plc Group.
All rights reserved. "NKJV" is a registered trademark
of International Bible Society.
UK trademark number 1448790.

Quotations marked KJV are from the Holy Bible,

King James Version.

ISBN Number: 978-1-64764-476-5

Cover Design: Allan Sealy

Dedication

I dedicate this book to all Brothers and Sisters in the Lord.

"But as many as received Him, to them gave He power to become the sons of God, even to them that believe on His name" John 1:12

Contents

Foreword	7
Jesus Christ, the believers thumb	9
Introduction	11
Remaining in Christ or staying connected	17
The work of the gardener	31
Productive and unproductive branches	37
How to stay connected to Christ	45
Bearing fruit	51
Fruits of the Spirit	81
Good fruit and bad fruit	91
Knowing the word	99
Eternal life	123
Self-control	133
Focus on Christ	143
Is Christ In Your Crisis?	219

Right location	287
Some of biblical characters of those who didn't stay connected	317
Conclusion	329

Foreword

This book is an enthusiastic celebration of the power of staying connected to Christ. It is also a unique tribute to the many teachings of Jesus Christ in chapter fifteen of John's gospel.

Another element of this book is that it provides many interesting biblical verses, of numerous biological and real life relevancies. In addition to that, there are innumerable scriptural vignettes that interweave bearing fruit as a Christian and staying connected to God. This book points out to the reader that this can only be achieved and sustained through faith, focus, trust and confidence in Christ and His Word.

Although the emphasis of this book is on abiding in Christ, it contains much that will be of interest to those outside the Church. It will also grip those who have a fascination of Christianity and want to have a simple, straight forward and realistic approach to the core values of its faith. Hopefully, these two groups of people will become productive branches in God's Kingdom.

The author has specially selected many relevant examples in real life to make comprehension of the subject matter precise and concise. Although these represent only a small fraction of the world of spiritual truth, they amply illustrate the high premium placed by the scriptures in the issues discussed. I think that the valuable contributions of this book to the great commission, pastoral ministry, and bearing the fruit of the spirit are crucial. Its underlying principle speaks to all generations and the unborn. The central message of the book can never be overstated, such is its importance. Therefore, I would recommend that this book be translated into many languages for global reading and discipleship.

Rev. Y SONG
Royal City Mission
London, England

Jesus Christ, The Believers Thumb

'....without Me, you can do nothing.'

These are the words of Jesus Christ recorded by John in John 15:5. It is part of the foundational Scriptures selected for this book. A Ghanaian proverb says "To tie a knot successfully, you need the thumbs." For believers He (Jesus) is our thumb without Him no Christian can succeed, this analogy shows that it is imperative to have Jesus Christ the Vine at the centre of your life.

Introduction

From the time God created man, He had wanted all his children to bear fruit. Remember what he commanded Adam and Eve in the Garden of Eden as Moses wrote; 'God blessed them and said unto them, "Be fruitful and increase in number; fill the earth and subdue it. Rule the fish of the sea and the birds of the air and over every living creature that live on the ground." Genesis 1: 28

This means that He expects all His children to bear fruit; He expects good things to come out of His children; their actions or fruitfulness that will bring glory to Him and he will reward them with His numerous blessings. This also means that God wants His children consistently to make progress in everything they do in life. This will only happen when His children remain in Him or in the context of this book, stay connected to the Vine, Jesus Christ who is God's only begotten Son through whom one can bear fruit. The point I am emphasising here is that without Him no one can do anything. You need to stay connected to Him; He gives you breath, health, strength and ability to attain and sustain these things. Paul said this when addressing the people of Athens: "For in him we live and move and have our being. As some of your own poets have said, "We are his offspring," Acts 17:28. In Him (Jesus Christ) we are all that we are and do whatever we do.

Paul who knows what God is to His children again said when he wrote to the people of Corinth, "Now he who supplies seed to the sower and bread for food will also supply and increase your store of seed and will enlarge the harvest of your righteousness," 2 Corinthians 9:10.

The problem is there are many believers today who do not know or understand what it means to remain in Christ, which is to stay connected to him in the context of this book which is the only way to bear fruit. John 15:5 highlights this through the words of Jesus about the importance of staying connected to Him. Its significance in a believer's life is why it is chosen as the title of this book.

Undoubtedly, I also believe there are many believers who may not know that it is expected of them to bear fruit when they are saved by Christ. This is why one of the biggest challenges facing many believers today is unfruitfulness; this means the failure to produce or to bear fruit for Christ. Compounding the situation is the fact that some people are producing fruit of very poor quality. This happens because they are doing it in a way, which the Lord does not approve of. Then there are those who will say that to please God or to be a Christian has nothing to do with being committed to Christ, or even going to church. They reduce the seriousness of abiding in Christ to the weak and overused phrase: 'Life is what you make it.' In other words, life depends on what one chooses to do, not as directed by God's word. This however points to mere 'spiritual laziness' and the failure to recognise the power of staying connected to Christ.

These people have no regard for the sanctity of the way prescribed by God through His word; others are selective about the rules by which they should live as a Christians. Many of them do this because it is self-serving and they have become a servant to their own desires rather than God's. These people create and justify their own standards for serving God. No wonder they are not receiving blessings or hearing from God. They are not fruitful because the line of communication is ruptured; the connection between them and the Lord has been severed. They are disconnected from the main source, which is Christ; they are trying to tie the knot without the thumb.

John 15:1-17, is the 'foundation Scripture' of this book and with other scriptures will be the basis on which I proclaim and teach the message of what it means to remain in Christ. I will constantly reinforce that without remaining in Christ, or staying connected to Him, no one can do anything good for Christ, himself or others. The truth of the matter is that a tree cannot bear fruit unless it is connected by its roots to the source of its food. In addressing the theme of this book, I will quote several proverbs and link my personal experiences to some of the topics for clarity and easier understanding.

Throughout the book, I will continue to ask provocative questions: "Do you know Him? What is your relationship with Him? Are you connected to Him or disconnected from Him?" Your answers to these questions are crucial as they hold the key to your meaningful existence on this earth. You may have everything materialistically but life without Christ is meaningless. Because of my passion for all men, both unbelievers and believers in Christ, I offer you these solutions through God's guidance and inspiration. To the glory of God, you are holding in your hands today what is the result of me staying connected to Him. Hallelujah! I am a pastor, preacher, a teacher of God's word and an author which, without Him it would have been impossible. In fact, I am glad to say that I am a good example of what the Lord can do through an ordinary man. Without Him, I cannot even imagine where I would have been now.

Remaining In Christ Or Staying Connected

The need to remain in Christ is, to stay connected to Him. The believer's relationship with Christ is one of total commitment and dependence on Him. This means to love Him with all your heart, your soul, your strength. This is a lifetime commitment and relationship with Him, there is no such thing as a day off, holidays or part time work when you are serving God. To remain in Christ you must stay connected to Him as it is a full time job and 24 hours a day business. Like a branch of a tree, you can only bear fruit only when you are present in Him at all times. This is a total separation from the world, living in Him and for Him. This means you must completely surrender your life to Him and serve Him only in the way recommended by Him. A songwriter says:

*"Lift up your eyes
Lift up your eyes to Jesus
Turn your back to the world
Lift up your eyes to Jesus."*

The reason you are to lift up your eyes to Jesus, turn your back on the devil and forsake the world is that the world has nothing to offer you but death. 'For the wages of sin *is* death, but the gift of God *is* eternal life in Christ Jesus our Lord.' Romans 6:23

This means that you have to redouble your efforts and focus on Him. Some believers are part committed, sometimes others are on a day off and on holidays. Some only come to Him when they have problems and need His help. These people live their lives how they want to, not as He commands as stated in the introduction. The true believer is a branch according to John 15:1-4 who deeply cements his relationship with Christ the Vine. Abiding in Christ is like the relationship between a pregnant woman and her child. When a fetus is in the womb, it is connected to its' mother through the umbilical cord. Through the cord, the fetus or baby receives oxygen for respiration, nutrients for growth and antibodies which help the baby to fight against any infection.

On the other hand, carbon dioxide and other waste substances move from the baby through the umbilical cord into the mother's blood. The mother's blood helps to carry this waste away so keeps the fetus system clean and healthy. So long as the fetus is connected to the mother's placenta, it will receive all the nutrients and oxygen it needs to survive and grow. The analogy clearly explains that if we stay connected to Jesus or remain in Him, we will receive His grace, His power, His word, and His direction. These will enable us to survive, grow and bear fruit to fulfill our obligation as believers because we are connected to Christ the Vine. When we are connected to Him, His blood will be able to flow through us and cleanse us from any waste or problems in our lives as the fetus must be connected to the mother at all times. Even when a child is born, it is still dependent on its mother; it stays connected to her, through breast-feeding and care.

In the same way, true believers stay connected to Christ as long as they live as He commands. This means that believers must be totally dependent on

Jesus Christ. In the Old Testament, the Bible says that "Unless the LORD builds the house, its builders labour in vain. Unless the LORD watches over the city, the watchmen stand guard in vain," Psalms 127:1. This means that a person is only established through his or her connection with God. This is in spite of what they have or what they can do. The Bible is not advocating against human effort nor is it encouraging idleness or laziness, what it is saying is that all men must come to the realisation that without Christ all that we have or what we can do is meaningless. Human efforts without God's help amounts to nothing. The further reading of the Scripture above indicates that to establish our families depends on God the builder of all lives. Never leave or abandon Christ in anything you do or undertake in life; for a city without God will always fail or crumble. Remain in Him, that is, stay connected to Him; the master craftsman, the life builder and your life will be stable. Always remember that whatever you want to do in life you must stay connected to Him for without Christ you can do nothing irrespective of your experience or knowledge.

It is for this reason that I was inspired to write this book, its chief objective is to encourage believers and unbelievers alike to stay connected to Christ. The subtext of its message is that we must stay connected in order to bear fruit. The strength of this message also creates the perfect platform for all believers to build our defences against the obstacles, which might want to impede our mission to be fruitful for Christ. I believe this is a powerful message; one I believe every Christian should adhere to. A message that has been inspired through the power of God; herein lies the foundation of this book, God's hands have guided it.

The power of this message is reinforced in John 1:3 (NKJV) which states, "All things were made through Him, and without Him nothing was made that was made." Also in Colossians 1:15-17, (NKJV) Paul too reinforces this, in verse 15 he states: "He is the image of the invisible God, the firstborn over all creation." In verse 16, he states, "For by Him all things were created that are in heaven and that are on earth, visible and invisible, whether thrones or dominions or principalities or powers. All things were created through Him and for Him." Verse 17 states, "And He is before all things, and in Him all things consist."

You may be working diligently to do your best in life but find that all your efforts are unsuccessful. The more you persevere the more things seem to go in opposition to your desired outcome. You try to work on your marriage but your spouse is getting more cantankerous in his or her attitude. You try to make peace with your neighbour or friend – no result. No matter how good the instructions you give your children they seem determined to going in the opposite direction.

You hold the same certificates as others but it seems your job applications are turned down wherever you present them. At this point, you say to yourself, "What am I going to do, where am I going wrong? What is going on? Is God asleep or something?" A sense of confusion grips you. You then pick the telephone to God, it rings and you get excited that it rings. A voice on the end announces, 'your service has been temporary disconnected, please settle any outstanding charges.' Those outstanding charges accumulated because you are disconnected. It is imperative that you settle your differences with Christ. Therefore, my advice to you is to re-connect to Him, Jesus Christ; the Vine and he will make you successful in every area of your life. The fact of the matter is when a branch is connected to the vine, it is saved because the vinedresser or the gardener takes care of the vine at all times.

Scripture shows the importance of this link, that we have come from Christ. Philippians 4:13: Paul said, "I can do everything through him who gives me strength." With Him, all things are possible. Also in his letter to the Corinthians church he said "Not that we are competent in ourselves to claim anything for ourselves, but our competence comes from God. He has made us competent as ministers of a new covenant not of the letter but of the Spirit; for the letter kills, but the Spirit gives life" 2 Corinthians 3:5-6. I wish brethren that all men would come to the same realization as Paul. That all that we have and whatever we can do in this world we owe everything to Him.

Paul is emphasizing in the above quotation that it is through God's enabling ability, which comes through remaining in Christ, which is staying connected to him that He has made us who we are. He furnishes us with the gifts of intellect, wisdom and the excellence of speech so we can be effective ministers of the gospel. It is through God's enabling ability that we ministers, get our skills, inspiration and strength to do what we do says Paul. We must always be mindful of this. Moses warned the Israelites not to be boastful about what they have but remember to honour God when he gives them rest in the Promised Land. Deuteronomy 8:17-18 states, "You may say to yourself, "My power and the strength of my hands have produced this wealth for me. But remember the LORD your God, for it is he who gives you the ability to produce wealth, and so confirms his covenant, which he swore to your forefathers, as it is today." There is a connection between the ability of God's power and being successful as a Christian. However, unless you bridge the gap between them you will not be rewarded. You need to know that your success depends on staying connected to God. This means that those who are boastful of what they have and do not attribute their success to God are making a big mistake. To accept that everything you have is down to the Lord you must affirm your relationship with Him in a covenant.

Without doubt, there are those who claim that they have made it or know someone who has made it without Christ. Now my brother, my sister before there is gravitation in your thinking, it is important to note that life does not end here on earth - it goes beyond eternity. I want you to know that material success on this earth does not mean you have made it. You can only say I have made it when you are connected to Jesus Christ the Vine, knowing that when you leave this earth you will live eternally with God and you recognise that He is the one with the power to offer you eternal life. More of staying connected to Christ to receive eternal life later in this book.

The Psalmist David wrote something to console those believers who may envy the lives of some unbelievers who have materially done better. He said, "Do not fret because of evil men or be envious of those who do wrong; for like the grass they will soon wither, like green plants they will soon die away. Trust in the Lord and do good; dwell in the land and enjoy safe pasture. Delight yourself in the Lord and he will give you the desires of your heart. Commit your way to the Lord; trust in him and he will do this: He will make your righteousness shine like the dawn, the justice of your cause like the noonday sun (Psalms 37:1-6). What the writer is saying here is that whatever unbelievers have is only for this lifetime. On Judgement day, they will end up in hell but what believers have leads to heaven and is eternal.

Later, I will illustrate how you can stay connected to Jesus Christ. I will also explain the required actions and rewards associated with two crucial paths to fruitfulness. My emphasis is that to remain in Christ is to stay connected to Him as seen is the context of this book. The believers must at all times be firmly connected to Christ the Vine to bear fruit. Just as a fetus or a baby is connected to its mother through the umbilical cord and as a productive branch, so must the believer keep an active line open to Christ at all times. It does not matter what the circumstances are, what is being stressed here is to remain in Christ as you take these actions:

- ✦ Focus on Him
- ✦ Have faith in Him

- ✦ Put your trust in Him
- ✦ Have confidence in Him
- ✦ Wait upon Him

In John 15:1-2, Jesus said, "I am the true vine, and my Father is the gardener. He cuts off every branch in me that bears no fruit, while every branch that does bear fruit he prunes so that it will be even more fruitful." This metaphor seeks to highlight the importance of bearing fruit and the relationship it has to the central theme of this book. The link here is that whatever we do it is crucial that we nourish and sustain our relationship with God through Christ. You do that by focusing and recognising the nature of your responsibility to God if you are to be fruitful with his blessings. It is vital that you show great interest in cultivating ways that are pleasing to God so that the fruits of your labour will produce positive action for his service. This will be reflected in the life you lead before God and man. The availability of his counsel is always there if you are having difficulty in your connection with God.

The metaphor in the above scripture again truly paints a picture of a concerned vine who wants to see the branches in him producing plenty fruit to please the gardener. Note also that the Vine distinguishes himself from other vines. Jesus who is the Vine declares his status quite emphatically; "I am the true vine" in the same way as He distinguishes Himself from other shepherds when He stated that, "I am the good shepherd" in John 10:11, 14. This is a statement of intention; ("I am the true vine") it wants the other plants to know it is the route to the main source of their growth. The other plants in the garden must be aware that other vines in the garden that would stunt their growth. The strength of this is shown through the role the gardener assigns to this vine. His job is to make sure that the source of strength and sustenance flows to the branches from him the main source. The plants in the garden can only bear fruit through the power of being connected to him the vine as he boldly states, "I am the vine; you are the branches. If a man remains in me and I in him, he will bear much fruit; apart from me you can do nothing" John 15:5 which is the opening Scripture of this book.

The strength to bear fruit comes directly from the vine. In other words, God wants all His servants to be productive but to be able to do so you must stay connected to the vine. This is to say God sent His Son Jesus Christ to be your strength, your guide so your works can flourish for God. He establishes the nature of the working relationship between you and Him. He also sends a clear message through His Son that those who fail to bear fruit will be thrown out of the garden. This is what Jesus states: "I am the vine; you are the branches. If a man remains in me and I in him, he will bear much fruit; apart from me you can do nothing. If anyone does not remain in me, he is like a branch that is thrown away and withers; such branches are picked up, thrown into the fire and burned," John 15: 5-6.

When you are in perfect harmony with Jesus you will be connected to God, but first you must proclaim your love for Him and remain faithful to his word. The main objective of doing these things is to reap the spiritual fruits of his blessings. The importance of this point means the metaphor of the gardener needs to be extended; Jesus speaks of himself as the Vine and God His Father as the Gardener. In this scenario, he sees those who claim to be Christians or followers of Him as branches. These branches represent two different types of Christians – First, the productive branches (those who bear fruit for Christ) and second, the unproductive branches (those who are not bearing any fruit for Christ).

One of the effects of the unproductive branches is that not only are they not bearing any fruit but they also infect, destroy and hinder other people from bearing fruit or coming to Christ. These unproductive believers can be seen as red ants (insects found mostly in tropical climates and inhabit trees that have fruits). Even though these red ants cannot eat the fruits they prevent others from eating them. You can see the striking similarity between the attitude of the reds ants and that of the unproductive believer. They are soul stealers who are attracted by the benefits and blessings that Christianity brings but are not prepared to work.

The Work Of The Gardener

Like every good gardener who wants his vineyard or garden to flourish, God has to carry out some pruning on His children (the branches in this context). In the process of the pruning, He cuts off the unproductive branches, which are not bearing fruit in order to make it easy for new growth elsewhere. The unproductive branches no longer meets the existing needs of the tree, so it has to be gotten rid of. He prunes the productive branches so that they can maximise guaranteed yields. This means that from God's perspective, pruning is good and beneficial for the productive branches. This is characterised by when God disciplines us in order to strengthen the fabric of our moral fibre and reinforce our faith. Extending this perspective, there is also direct correlation between God's action as the gardener and Jesus' role as the vine.

It is their co-operation, which maintains order in the garden (Christendom) and eliminates weeds (unproductive believers) which impedes the progress of successful fruit bearing. We must stay connected to Jesus Christ, the Vine in order to be part of God's master plan of the production cycle.

Pruning is also crucial to the fruit bearing process; when you cut off or trim branches of trees, it creates stronger growth or increases yield and capacity. A tree that is pruned prepares and makes way for new shoots to grow and become branches. Invariably productive believers have to surrender their vices, examine their own faults, know where the fault lines lie in relation to temptation and throw themselves on God's mercy so he can rectify their imperfections. If a tree is not getting the correct nutrients, enough water or sunshine, then all these things would affect the completion of its productive cycle. Therefore, it is important that we as Christians should continuously live an upright life before God and man. In doing so this places us in a prime position to win more souls for Christ; this is very a much part of our fruit bearing process.

These are the reasons Christ died on the cross, to give us an opportunity to redeem ourselves, to intercede on our behalf, to bear fruit for His father's Kingdom. The reward God has in store for us is eternal life so it is imperative that we obey His word. This way we are able to look within ourselves to see what part of our character or life needs pruning. Quite often, we want to sit in judgement of ourselves as to the status of our fruit bearing; but it is quite evident when a tree is not bearing fruit. Many Christians talk a good talk, walk a good walk but have nothing to show for it.

God has a stark warning for the field (the unproductive believer) which is not bearing fruit; he will not waste time pruning it. He warns us: "I will lay it waste; it shall not be pruned or dug, but there shall come up briers and thorns. I will also command the clouds that they rain briers and throngs," Isaiah 5:6 (NKJV). This is a warning to all those who half-heartedly commit themselves to living in the way that he commands them to live. Those who think they can fool God with their empty gestures of good platitudes. If your works are not connected to Jesus the Vine, then they are without substance; God the Gardener will not reward you accordingly. You have to demonstrate your worth to Him by the life you lead and cannot do or hide it under false pretences. We must also recognize that the nature of the relationship we have in this whole process of bearing fruit for God. This recognition is important to the way we approach our Christian walk and the way we will be rewarded. Bearing fruit is not only a necessity but a required action if we want God to fulfill His promise to us. In this relationship, God expects total commitment, faithfulness, trust, honesty; these are the crucial nutrients needed to accelerate your growth in Christ so you can be bountiful in harvest.

My parents were farmers so I know the importance of pruning. In most cases, farmers found it very difficult to cut some of the braches of some crops such as cocoa and coffee. They also struggled when cutting out or removing some of the planted things like corn, cocoyam, plantains etc. The fact of the matter is cutting or removing some of this vegetation gives way for the remaining ones to have greater strength to grow. In other words pruning enables them to produce a better crop yield. Failure to do so affects production.

In the process of pruning, some people and habits have to be dropped or be cut out. A believer who wants to live to produce better fruits and maximize his fruits must cut and remove some of these habits and people from their lives. I would not have been where I am today, doing what I am doing if some people were still with me. I cried for the departure of some people from my life because at a human being level I thought they were in my life to save me. The opposite was true as they were wishing for my downfall. Some friends and habits are dream killers; they will hinder the progress of your growth. If you find it challenging you must enlist God's help so you can purge them out of your life. It is worth doing as these habits and people always hinder a believer from reaching his or her fruit bearing capacity or potential. Prune your life now and you will be who God created you to be.

Productive And Unproductive Branches

In Jeremiah 17:5-8, the prophet makes a sharp contrast between two types of people, those who put their trust in man who is the barren or the unproductive ones. They are cursed because they put their trust in man and rely on the flesh as their strength; their heart has departed from the Lord because they are disconnected. Whereas the people who are fruitful and productive will not fear the heat when the sun comes out; their leaves will remain green and they will not be anxious in the year of drought. Furthermore, they will not cease from yielding fruit. These people are like a tree that is planted by the waters which spreads out its roots by the river to get to the source of its growth. In this context, they are connected to God who symbolizes the river in the aforementioned Scripture. When one is in constant contact with

God he draws on the spiritual nutritious strength to produce fruit needed for him or for others also because fruits are seen and benefit not only the producer but others too.

From John 15, as we saw earlier Jesus said that there are two branches, two types of believers connected to Him the Vine, the productive and the unproductive ones. In verse 2, He said "Every branch in Me that does not bear fruit He takes away; and every branch that bears fruit He prunes, that it may bear more fruit." (NKJV) Jesus re-emphasized this when in Matthew 7:21-23 when he also said: "Not everyone who says to Me, 'Lord, Lord,' shall enter the kingdom of heaven, but he who does the will of My Father in heaven. Many will say to Me in that day, 'Lord, Lord, have we not prophesied in Your name, cast out demons in Your name, and done many wonders in Your name?" And then I will declare to them: 'I never knew you; depart from Me, you who practice lawlessness!' Matthew 7:21-23 (NKJV). To bear good fruit or to be productive means to excel in anything you do either for the Lord, yourself or and for others. When you are unproductive, it means that you have failed to reach your true potential for God, yourselves and others. It is especially more telling when you fail to use your gifts and talents to serve God. You cannot be a productive branch without being connected to Christ. He reminds us "without me you can do nothing." Therefore, as you read this book I implore you to examine yourself to see if you are connected to him. Do you want to be fruitful or productive in your work, your marriage or in your relationship with others? First, you must be planted by the river of God and be well watered. Once you are connected, you will receive strength and direction to bear fruit in due season as the prophet said.

Remember "The Song of the Vineyard" in (Isaiah 5:1-7)

Now let me sing to my Well-beloved a song of my Beloved regarding His vineyard: My Well-beloved has a vineyard on a very fruitful hill. He dug it up and cleared out its stones, and planted it with the choicest vine. He built a tower in its midst, and also made a winepress in it; So He expected *it* to bring forth *good* grapes, But it brought forth wild grapes. "And now, O inhabitants of Jerusalem and men of Judah, Judge, please, between Me and My vineyard. What more could have been done to My vineyard That I have not done in it? Why then, when I expected *it* to bring forth *good* grapes, Did it bring forth wild grapes? And now, please let Me tell you what I will do to My vineyard: I will take away its hedge, and it shall be burned; *And* break down its wall, and it shall be trampled down. I will lay it waste; It shall not be pruned or dug, But there shall come up briers and thorns. I will also command the clouds that they rain no rain on it." For the vineyard of the LORD of hosts *is* the house of Israel, And the men of Judah are His pleasant plant. He looked for justice, but behold, oppression; For righteousness, but behold, a cry *for help.* Isaiah 5:1-7 (NKJV)

In the quotations above it is clear to see that any other gardener or farmer would have expected good fruit like the expectation of the gardener (God) in John 15. In the context of the above narrative the gardener was greatly disappointed having spent time, energy and resources to prepare his vineyard. He anticipated good fruits but got bad he probably questioned why when he expected a good harvest of grapes and why the yield was bad. In other words, he looked for justice, but saw bloodshed, righteousness, but heard cries of distress. These are the character of people who even though they have seen Christ yet choose to be led by the flesh instead of the spirit. They lead an unworthy life, which Paul said should not even be spoken among believers. This is what he wrote to the Galatians in Galatians 5:19-21 (NKJV), "Now the works of the flesh are evident, which are: adultery, fornication, uncleanness, lewdness, idolatry, sorcery, hatred, contentions, jealousies, outbursts of wrath, selfish ambitions, dissensions, heresies, envy, murders, drunkenness, revelries, and the like; of which I tell you beforehand, just as I also told *you* in time past, that those who practice such things will not inherit the kingdom of God. The Lord hates those who bear such bad fruits for they allowed the world to blasphemy against God. (2 Samuel 12:14)

In Romans 2:23-24 Paul states, "You who make your boast in the law, do you dishonor God through breaking the law? For the name of God is blasphemed among the Gentiles because of you" (NKJV). Stay connected to the Vine (Jesus) at all times. The Gardener (the Lord) will prune you to bear more fruits, blessings and the power to stay connected. It is imperative that you bear good fruit, sweet fruits to bring glory to God as bad fruits allow the enemies of God to blaspheme against Him, this is something the Lord detests. A stark warning exist for those who fail to bear good fruit - you will be cut off, separated or disconnected from the Lord and thrown into fire. When this happens, you become vulnerable and will have no protection of the Gardener (the Lord) as He warned in Isaiah 5:5-6, "Now I will tell you what I am going to do to my vineyard; I will take away its hedge, and it will be destroyed; I will break down its wall, and it will be trampled. I will make it a wasteland, neither pruned nor cultivated, and briers and thorns will grow there. I will command the clouds not to rain on it." Imagine the danger it will be for anyone if God the Gardener removed his hedge from around you then demolished the protective wall around you. This will dangerously expose you to all destructive elements of Satan and his desires.

This can happen when a believer fails to bear fruit because he is disconnected, lost protection and care from God the gardener. Jesus said in Matthew 5:13 (NKJV) "...but if the salt loses its flavour, how shall it be seasoned? It is then good for nothing but to be thrown out and trampled underfoot by men." This is a man who has discontinued believing the Good News and has gone back to his worldly ways. He returns to the same things he once condemned as evil. His wretched situation is completed as he loses respect for himself and that of those around him.

Do not believe those who say that Christianity is just about your heart and that one can do it one's own way. You must also be very watchful of those who propagate that you can be a Christian without Christ or without going to Church. This is a smart lie from the Devil designed to deceive you; it is impossible to do anything without God or the Spirit. The emphasis here is to stay connected; you can and will be a productive branch that bears good fruit. Everyone who professes to be a follower of Christ but bears bad and sour fruit brings shame to God and himself. He also allows the enemies of God to speak against God. If Christ is glorified through the good fruit you bear you will receive the benefit of staying connected to him.

How To Stay Connected To Christ

Now someone may ask, "How can I remain in Christ? How can I stay connected to Christ in order to bear good fruit that will bring glory to God the Father and will enable me to receive the benefit of staying connected to Him?" If this is your heart desire then I think the following points could be of a help. I think it is good to know how you can stay connected to Him. Even though some believers may not agree, The Apostolic Church Tenet number ten states, "The possibility of falling from grace" that is, it is possible for a believer to fall from the grace of God, in the context of this book I would say: the possibility of disconnecting from Him as a believer is possible if care is not taken. The point I am trying to make here is that failure to remain in Him can result in one falling from the Grace of God that is, being disconnected from Him.

To receive Jesus as Lord and Saviour is the first contact to remain in Him. John maintains that to remain in Christ is to receive him as Lord and Saviour, which is to believe in His name, (John 1:12) says: "But as many as received Him, to them He gave the right to become children of God, to those who believe in His name".

Jesus also reinforces the same principle about being born again in John 3:3-5 (NKJV) Jesus answered and said to him, "Most assuredly, I say to you, unless one is born again, he cannot see the kingdom of God." Nicodemus said to Him, "How can a man be born when he is old? Can he enter a second time into his mother's womb and be born?" Jesus answered, "Most assuredly, I say to you, unless one is born of water and the Spirit, he cannot enter the kingdom of God". John goes further when he said, "Whoever confesses that Jesus is the Son of God, God abides in him, and he in God". (1 John 4:15). Having faith in Jesus and believing that he is God's Son connects you to both of him and his father. This simply means that everyone became part of the branches of the Vine and children of God when they received Christ as Lord and Saviour; it also means that they must believe in his name. The Scripture reinforces this when it says, "That if you confess with your mouth, "Jesus is Lord," and believe in your heart that God raised him from the dead, you will be saved. For it is with your heart that you believe and are justified, and it is with your mouth that you confess and are saved." Romans 10:9-10

"You are all sons of God through faith in Christ Jesus, for all of you who were baptised into Christ have clothed yourselves with Christ. There is neither Jew nor Greek, slave nor free, male nor female, for you are all one in Christ Jesus." Galatians 3:26-28

Once you have received God in your life through Christ Jesus you must also stay connected to Him, you must also obey his commandments. There is no option of picking and choosing the ones you wish to obey. You are subject to His rules and must do what the master requires whether His rules seem favourable or not. The Bible states, "For as many as are led by the Spirit of God, these are sons of God". Romans 8:14 (NKJV) To be led by the Spirit is to be controlled by the Spirit and that is doing what the Spirit tells you, following the instructions God gives you through His word.

The truth of the matter is Jesus is not only the Savior, as many know but also Lord whose commandments we must all obey that will keep you connected to Him. The Bible says that, "Now he who keeps His commandments abides in Him, and He in him. And by this we know that He abides in us, by the Spirit whom He has given us" 1 John 3:24 (NKJV). When we receive Christ as our saviour, we must also know that He is our Lord. Therefore, we should ask Him to take his rightful position as Lord over our lives obeying Him in all our daily activities. Unfortunately, many are happy to be called Christians, they go to church every Sunday or any other day but when it comes to living according to the precepts of God they will like to do their own thing. In fact they live lives, which are not worthy of God's children, this is why many cannot stay connected to Christ, because you cannot successfully connect to Him while you do your own thing.

Furthermore, to be able to remain in Him you must continue to believe the good news, that is, you must live by the word of God. The importance of staying connected to Christ through the word of God is one aspect of bearing fruit, which cannot be ignored. It is easy to discontinue believing the good news, which is to discontinue believing that Jesus Christ is God's Son who died for our sins. It is also easy to forget He was raised to give us new life, and that He returned to the Father to establish His Kingdom and to prepare a place for those who will believe on his name. This means that there is a possibility that someone might forsake his first love for Christ due to many reasons including temptations from the Devil. This could also happen through receiving bad doctrines from false teachers of God's word and the person's personal love of the world.

Many of you reading this book will bear me witness that the love you had for the Lord and his word has gone cold in you. It is obvious that you are losing connection with Him and if nothing is done eventually, you will be disconnected totally. The great Apostle John knew this fact when he wrote to advise his readers urging them never to forget this basic truth (the good news) they heard from the beginning. He also encourages that as long as you hold on to this belief you will remain in Christ and he in you. He said: "Therefore let that abide in you which you heard from the beginning. If what you heard from the beginning abides in you, you also will abide in the Son and in the Father." 1 John 2:24 (NKJV). Someone who is familiar with this quotation interprets it this way; He says that his life is hidden in Christ whose life is also hidden in God the Father, as proclaimed by the Scripture, in this context, it would be impossible for any harm to come near him. As it is difficult to separate Christ from God, therefore it would be an impossible task getting at this person. It is difficult because Christ is intertwined with that person, Christ has become a fortified protective shield for him. If you continue to believe the Good News, Jesus is the Son of God, why He had to die, His resurrection and His second coming then your salvation is assured and you will be able to stay connected to Him and these beliefs will help you to bear fruit.

Bearing Fruit

As I indicated in the introduction, man was created for progress, he was created for good works, and therefore, God expects his children to bear fruit. I have recently come to know that many believers are only aware of soul winning as fruit bearing by believers. It is clear in John 15:1-17 and other scriptures that unlike the unproductive branches who will be cut off and burn by fire God expects all of His children (the productive branches) who remain in Him or stay connected to Him to bear the other fruits. As well that will bring glory to Him and that will enable Him to bless His children. God expects His children to be fruitful and productive in every area of their lives. This productive life should be progressive and continuous to bring glory to God the Father, the gardener in this context. Now let us move on to discuss some of these fruits God expects from His children based on the theme quotation chosen for this book and a few others.

The fruit of answered prayers

John 15:7 states, "If you remain in me and my words remain in you, ask whatever you wish, and it will be given you". We see that the importance of staying connected to Christ is clearly shown here; God will not tolerate unfruitfulness. He has established His purpose and it must be carried out His way. The source of being connected to Him (God) is Jesus Christ the true Vine. When you have a connection with Jesus, your harvest will be bountiful; your spiritual and material needs will be met. When you abide in Him, the countenance of His blessings will illuminate your face, strengthen your life e.g. your marriage, heal your broken relationships and you will be empowered to bear fruits of answered prayer—First, there must be recognition that to fulfil these things, you must remain in Him and follow His plan.

Prayer is one of the many ways of remaining or staying connected to Christ, the theme of this book. Jesus promised those who will remain in Him or stay connected to Him and His words to grant them answers to their prayers. The question is, why is it that many prayers which believers offer to God go unanswered? In John 15:7, Jesus offers the recipe to the fruit of answered prayers. He is stating that after you have received Him as your Lord and personal Savior that guarantees you becoming his branch, it is not enough to grant you answers to your prayers. If you want His father (the Gardener) to give you anything you desire in your prayers, the keys are, He said:

1. If you abide in Me, and
2. My words abide in you

This means that if you receive him into your heart, you must also live by His word. Because prayer is one of the most important things in the life of every believer, I believe it is very important to know how our prayers can be answered, because praying without answers is a waste of time and energy and discouragement for a believer. Therefore, these words of Jesus Christ must be taking seriously. Due to lack of answered prayers many believers: have lost interest in praying, others find prayers to be boring and tiring. For others prayer is no longer a spiritual exercise but a mere recitation of words or a tradition without any spiritual meaning or advantage. As a result, these people pray but with no expectations. On the contrary, those who know and believe that God listens and answers the prayer of His children they pray with passion; and always look forward to having an answer to their prayers.

It is better to know how to receive answer to prayer because when believers receive answers to their prayer it increases the person's faith. It intensifies his or her relationship and connection with God. Jesus made a promise to believers; He said, "If you will remain in me" - which means to stay connected to him - anything you ask for will be given to you. It is also clear from Jesus' statement that before anyone prays, he or she must make sure that the prayers is built on the foundations of the word of God (the bible). The believer has to know that God will only answer a prayer that is based on his word. This has to be the case because it is from His word that God reveals His will and the promises to his children. When prayer is offered to God based on His word it puts Him in remembrance of what he has said. God is only bound to answer prayer when it is based on his word.

It is unfortunate that some people have more confidence in the words of people. They take the words of these people more seriously than God's word, which is always certain to produce whatever it says. We believe in and pay for some medicines, which sometimes bring more trouble; we even pay for the promises of man which in most cases fail. People do not always intentionally fail you, sometimes it is beyond their control. I know many Ghanaian parents who would have wanted to further the education of their children or to help them to learn a special trade. These skills would have given their children a brighter future but they could not afford to help them. Many times, I have personally tried to help people, but could not, because I did not have the means to do so. Jesus says that if you want Him (the Vine) to feed you and answer your prayers; you must stay connected to Him, let His words remain in you.

Christianity is not a casual thing; it is a total life commitment to Christ and feeding on God's word everyday. Anyone whose eyes are on Jesus and feeds on His word day and night will always pray as required by God's law. These prayers will always produce a good result. Many prayers are not answered because those who offered them are those who have no relationship with Christ, the unproductive branches and the unstable believers. Apostle John said, "Now this is the confidence that we have in Him, that if we ask anything according to His will, He hears us. And if we know that He hears us, whatever we ask, we know that we have the petitions that we have asked of Him," 1 John 5:14-15 (NKJV) stay connected to Him and you will bear the fruit of receiving answers to every prayer you offer to Him.

God has promised to answer the prayers of his children; many quotations affirm that, but for our prayers to be answered or be fruitful it is very important we know the will of God in our lives. So that we can pray to God in accordance to that will, or else we will be wasting time praying without getting any result, our prayers will be fruitless. No matter how much you want or desire what you are praying for; your grieving, even how many days you fast and pray the Lord will only answer prayers in accordance with his will. Many prayers go unanswered simply because they are not in line with God's divine will.

Someone may ask, "How will I know the will of God in order to pray according to that will?" God's will is his divine purpose in the life of his children and that divine purpose is always in line with what he has said in his word, God's will is what pleases him. Since no one has ever seen God, only through his word, I will say, God's will is simply his word, the divine scripture. When we are knowledgeable of his word, we know the will of God. As the will of man is a written document, so also God's will for man is his written word, the Bible.

The reason why God will always answer prayers offered to him according to His will or His word is that He is bound by his will or his word. Simply the apostle is saying when you know the will of God which is his word you have confidence to go to Him in prayer knowing that whatever you ask you will receive because it is in accordance with His will. He says, "If you remain in me and my words remain in you, ask whatever you wish, and it will be given you".

The fruit of joy

John 15:11 says, "I have told you this so that my joy may be in you and that your joy may be complete." In this verse Jesus told His disciples that they will be joyful, happy or delightful at all times irrespective of the circumstances so long as they hold on to his words. This is so because His words bring comfort to the heart. Paul demonstrates this to his readers in prison when he wrote to the people of Philippi. He states, "Rejoice in the Lord always. Again I will say, rejoice! Let your gentleness be known to all men. The Lord is at hand. Be anxious for nothing, but in everything by prayer and supplication, with thanksgiving, let your requests be made known to God; And the peace of God, which surpasses all understanding, will guard your hearts and minds through Christ Jesus." Philippians 4:4-7 (NKJV)

How could a man in prison be telling or preaching to others about joy? He could do that because of his connection with Jesus. This joy is not about what is happening, as in the case of happiness but it is faith in God. The word of God brings joy to the heart so remain in Him and feed on His words. Therefore, you will not be anxious at the slightest hint of trouble. God's word is well able to produce anything that it says it will.

You must become familiar with the conditions set by God when bearing fruit for Christ, as these conditions are not up for discussion. You must come to terms with what is involved because God as head of the vineyard has no time for timewasters. He wants people who are prepared to go into battle to win souls for His kingdom and bring glory to His name. Therefore, you have to be equipped in order to do these things effectively. Jesus categorically states that no one can bear any of these fruits unless they remain in him. In other words, no one can produce any of these fruits using their own ability; they must be connected to Him who is the vine.

The fruit of love

John 15:12 says: "This is My commandment, that you love one another as I have loved you". There is an important aspect to any connection, a bond must exist; the tapestry that binds the forces together. It is a required component of a network if there is going to be effective communication; in this context, Jesus is the vine of love. Love is one of the greatest fruits expected from every believer; this is to have strong or deep affection, tender towards God and our fellow human beings. God demonstrates His love towards men when he gave his only son. Scripture states, "For God so loved the world that He gave His only begotten Son, that whoever believes in Him should not perish but have everlasting life" John 3:16 (NKJV). Again, in Romans 5:8 (NKJV) Paul said, "But God demonstrates His own love toward us, in that while we were still sinners, Christ died for us." His Son Jesus Christ, transports our messages and prayers to Him. God wants peace amongst his believers because if we are busy fighting and backstabbing each other, there is no time to bear fruit for Him. He knows it is Satan's plan to steal our time in this way so it is imperative to love one another as love conquers all things. It dissipates the depth of our anger; it disintegrates the hatred that often threatens to consume us and dispels the envy in our hearts. How can we love God and hate our fellow men as the Scripture says in 1 John 4:20-21 (NKJV), "If someone says, "I love God," and hates his brother, he is a liar; for he who does not love his brother whom he has seen, how can he love God whom he has not seen? And this commandment we have from Him: that he who loves God must love his brother also."

It is the work of the Devil when people hate each other so Jesus commands us to use love to defeat these things. These things are the greatest obstacles to us bearing fruit. Bearing fruit is our reason to prove that we are connected to Christ the Vine. Love is the strongest antidote to envy, hatred, covetousness, greed and anger and it covers a multitude of sin. These are the weeds that impede growth and accelerate the prospect of barrenness. Abiding or remaining in Him produces the fruit of love. To bear the fruit of love as Jesus had already said believers must first abide in His love "If you keep My commandments, you will abide in My love, just as I have kept My Father's commandments and abide in His love." John 15:10 (NKJV) So, you see, before one can bear the fruit of love, you must first keep his commandments which is a recording of His words in the Scriptures.

The Scripture states that Jesus commanded his disciples and all his followers to love one another as he has first loved them. He said, "A new commandment I give to you, that you love one another; as I have loved you, that you also love one another. By this all will know that you are My disciples, if you have love for one another." John 13:34-35 (NKJV)

For Jesus to say I give His disciples a new commandment, there must have been an older commandment related to love which is found in Leviticus 19:18 (NKJV) Where the Bible states: "You shall not take vengeance, nor bear any grudge against the children of your people, but you shall love your neighbour as yourself: I am the Lord."

Also in Matthew 22:34-40 Jesus recommended love as one of the greatest commandments. In giving new commandments to his disciples, Jesus is telling them and all believers that they should love each other as he has first loved them. By doing this, they will be demonstrating His unconditional and sacrificial love to one another. I will always maintain that there are many people who if told that they have to feed and clothe others as themselves, then countless desperate people will die of hunger and go out without clothes. This is true, because some of these same individuals hardly buy food or clothes for themselves. They make it a problem for themselves because they would rather save money in the bank, just for the sake of it. On the contrary, loving the way Jesus loved, paints quite a different picture - that is, you do good to your neighbour unconditionally; which means that you do it to others, even if you do not do it for yourself.

Paul gives strong admonitions and specific recommendations about love in the context of its application to bearing fruit. The 'resounding gong or a clanging cymbal' is a metaphor for empty and useless noises which equates to not bearing fruit. In 1 Corinthians 13:1-8, Paul states that without love whatever we do as believers will be worthless. This also includes if you are operating in the power of the gifts of the Holy Spirit. It is important that you know this, because love is the basis on which all the gifts of the Spirit must operate. Love is at the heart of fruit bearing because you need love to carry out the works of Jesus Christ. Jesus is the very essence of love and if you are connected to him, you will have the strength of character to transform your life for his service. However, if love is not embedded in your works you get no rewards.

The Scripture makes it clear that love is not only what you say, but it must be followed up by a corresponding action, which demonstrates that your words matches your action. Many people state that they can love but their actions contradict what they proclaim. There is a story told about two friends traveling through a forest on foot. In the middle of their conversation one of them called Kwame asked his friend Kwaku, "Do you really love me?" Kwame asked Kwaku this question three times. Kwaku answered, "Yes" each time but Kwame was not convinced. Trying to gain reassurance, Kwame queried Kwaku's sincerity the third time asking "Are you sure?" This is similar to the scenario when Jesus asked Peter three times, "Do you love me?' and the Bible asserts that Peter was hurt by Jesus' question as demonstrated in John 21:15-18. In the early part of this story, Kwaku was also indignant about the nature of his friend's question. He swore an oath of allegiance to prove his love for his friend. In the oath he pledged that he will even die for him if he has to.

Whilst they continued, talking and walking a big lion suddenly appeared-roaring viciously as it sped towards them. Fortunately, for Kwaku he was good at tree climbing so he ran and climbed the nearest tree to escape, leaving his friend behind. Not a few moments before he had pledged that he would die for him to prove his love, now, the vulnerable Kwame who could not climb the a tree as quickly decided to lie down, hold his breath and pretend as if he was dead. The lion jumped on him and after some seconds, it placed its mouth to his ears as if it was telling him something and then left without doing anything to harm him. Quickly Kwaku got down from the tree, ran to his friend and asked, "When I was up on the tree I saw that the lion told you something; what was it?"

Looking him in the eye, Kwame reminded him of the oath he made and his actions when the lion appeared. Kwame then told him that the lion said he was not a true friend and warned him about keeping company with him. Kwame told him: "You only say you love me in words but you have not proved it with your action today so this marks the end of our friendship." Like Kwaku many people are contrary to the real characteristic of love; Kwaku said he loved his friend Kwame and was even ready to die for him, but could not demonstrate it when the need arose.

Jesus Christ demonstrated what real love is with His atoning death for mankind when He died to save us. With Him, believers can also demonstrate the same sacrificial love to our brothers and sisters in the Lord, our friends and our neighbors. Do it, not only with our mouth but also with a corresponding action. Do you just say you love others, your wife or husband or you do really mean what you say from your heart? Do it with the fruit of love, the Jesus type of love. As a Pastor and counselor, I have had many women complain bitterly to me that their husbands would only express their love for them when they need them to satisfy their sexual passion. On the other hand, men also complained their wives only demonstrated love for them when they need something from them in return. Similarly, many people will demonstrate love to others when they want something in return. In this case, I ask myself this question, "Is this really love or a pretended love?" Jesus' type of love is the one produced by those who are connected to Him, which is love not based on what you say but more importantly, about what you do - it is sacrificial. Years ago a Ghanaian Christian music artist wrote a song entitled "In Him Is Life." The song states that when Jesus Christ saw death approaching mankind He ran ahead to face death and died instead to save mankind. His action demonstrated love in the fullest sense of the word.

The fruit of soul winning and soul

In John 15: 16 (NKJV) Jesus says: 'You did not choose Me, but I chose you and appointed you that you should go and bear fruit, and that your fruit should remain, that whatever you ask the Father in My name He may give you'.

This verse is one that points to the fact that being born into God's family is not merely about going to heaven. There are other purposes: bearing fruits, of bringing people to Christ and ensuring they will stay. Failure to do so as a believer would make you an unproductive branch as supported by Jesus who said: "Every branch in Me that does not bear fruit He takes away". Perhaps and undoubtedly the most popular known form of fruit bearing for many believers is soul winning. There is another aspect which may be unknown to many, but is quite clear in this verse; it is crucial that the souls won should remain. It is waste of time and energy if our fruits fail to remain. John states if a person is well and truly connected to Christ he or she will bear these fruits and reap the benefits of doing so. Some of the benefits for doing this are that your prayers and petitions will be answered as it is stated in

John 15:7. Answered prayer comes from knowing, believing and practicing the word of God.

There is great joy in knowing that God listens and answers your prayer. The joy of answered prayers comes from being contented, being at peace and being at one with the Lord and Saviour, Jesus Christ. This joy will only reach you if you are connected to the Vine, Jesus Christ. He is the only one who can transfer this powerful medicine for the healing of your psychological and physical ailments. He is the channel through which all good things must pass to reach the core of your happiness and fulfilment. This joy is also connected to winning souls and the retention of those souls; in essence, you are responding to the Great Commission of Jesus Christ to bring people into the kingdom. Matthew 28:19-20 19 (NKJV) states, "Go therefore and make disciples of all the nations, baptizing them in the name of the Father and of the Son and of the Holy Spirit, teaching them to observe all things that I have commanded you; and lo, I am with you always, even to the end of the age." Amen. It is true you cannot be a true witness for someone or represent them in a case unless you know that person or forensic details of the case. In any other circumstances, your representation will be under false pretences. Similarly, you cannot represent or effectively witness for Christ unless you are connected to Him. In addition, there must also be an unconditional belief in Him and His word.

It is my uttermost pleasure and desire to witness, preach or teach about Christ because of my connection with Him. I am always honored when He uses me to bring others to Him. The fullness of my joy is when I see these people stay in Him. I thank God that by His grace many people have come to know and stay in Christ through me. I remember one particular young boy years ago who came to Christ through me when I used to be a youth leader. This boy was from a very poor background. His life reflected that of someone from a typical village in Africa whose family is poor and do not have proper footwear or clothes. The most sad part of this boy's situation is that he became the subject of ridicule in the town where he lived. He was called all sorts of names and no one respected him. To God's glory when he came to know Christ and became a member of my witness movement, after becoming my disciple for some years Jesus transformed his life to the point that people no longer ridiculed him or call him names. Before we parted from each other, he had become a preacher and a true witness for Christ who saved him. Suffice to say he also enhanced his quality of life by engaging in petty trading to support himself. This transformation earned him great respect from others. This is what Jesus can do through every believer - the transforming of lives if we will respond to the Great Commission by bringing people to Him.

Every believer young or old must know that it is his or her primary objective to bring people to Christ. In addition, to make sure that these souls stay and become rooted in him because this is the reason why every believer was born into Christ's family. For more information about how easily you can bear the fruit of soul winning, I recommend you read my book, "Be Ye Transformed".

Good example in the world

In Matthew 5:13-16 Jesus clearly states, "You are the salt of the earth; but if the salt loses its flavor, how shall it be seasoned? It is then good for nothing but to be thrown out and trampled underfoot by men. You are the light of the world. A city that is set on a hill cannot be hidden. Nor do they light a lamp and put it under a basket, but on a lamp stand, and it gives light to all who are in the house. Let your light so shine before men, that they may see your good works and glorify your Father in heaven". (NKJV) Your works as a Christian must be accompanied by faith, which is the currency you need in order to be, and stay connected to the source of your salvation - Jesus Christ the Vine. Christians are to reflect Christ in their everyday lives to bring glory to God through their relationship with him. This relationship must be a productive one; one which enhances the lives of others and bring glory to His name.

The fruit of salt

Salt, is a special tasteful substance that gives taste to food and is used as preservative for food and meat. In Ghana today, some meat and fish are still been preserved with salt. Without salt, food becomes tasteless and difficult to eat it. There was a man who was asked by a doctor not to use salt because of a health condition. In trying to be clever, the man always used dried fish in his soup. The fish was preserved with salt, so it still had a high salt content. Unknown to the man his health was deteriorating instead of improving. During his check-up the doctor asked him if he was using salt. He told the doctor he no longer used salt but put dried fish in his soup. This shows the importance of salt for a man to risk his life to eat it - he is one of many people who risk their lives by using too much salt. Because of its importance in the life of mankind, it is said that the salt on earth represents the good people and many people including Christians believe that they are the salt of the world. It is true they are the salt of the world, we give the world a good taste and we preserve the world. Jesus reaffirms this to his disciples and all believers when He said, "You are the salt of the earth." Even most unbelievers and people of other faiths expect Christians to do good at all times because of our connection with Christ. He is the best person that has ever lived: believe it or not, accept it or not he is a man who has never sinned even though He offended many because of His truth. That is the reason He never said sorry or apologised to anyone when He was on earth. So you see, your role as Christians is very crucial for the preservation of God's plan here on earth; you are the very reason for its sustenance. You are charged with a responsibility to make sure His people are fed the right foods, given the right nutrients, follow the correct morals and values; this means that you must have substance in order to have any credibility with God. And all your efforts will be wasted if you do not avail yourself to Him as your work will lack gravitas (a serious and impressive attitude or way of behaving); your words will be empty, your victories will be hollow, your tasks will not produce meaningful results; you wouldn't be connected to the source of your life as a believer. You need to make sure your works are seasoned with God's power and will; otherwise, you will lose favour with Him. Jesus said if a Christian loses his salty flavour, he is good for nothing, "But if the salt loses its flavor, how shall it be seasoned? It is then good for nothing but to be thrown out and trampled underfoot by men." (Matthew 5:13)

This means that the presence of believers must produce a 'good taste' such as peace and harmony not war and discord. People must feel safe and protected in the midst of believers, because they are fruit of salt like Jesus Christ our Lord. However, you can only produce salty fruit and remain salty when you remain in Him. To maintain this you must be very careful at all times, about what you do or say. You must always portray and seek to bring good flavour to your works everywhere you go.

Another way to maintain your saltiness is to cautiously choose those who you associate with. An old expression states: "Birds of the same feather flock together." Your association with others can either help or damage your good reputation. Do not forget what Jesus said about losing your salty flavour. It is also similar to what Peter said about a dog going back to its vomit (2 Peter 2:22) a very disgusting scene indeed. Jesus reinforces Peter's position when he again states, "And the final condition of that man is worse than the first." Matthew 12:45. I have seen and heard about many people whose lives have fallen in disarray after they have backslidden or turned away from God. They have gone back into the world to lap up the same vomit they once scorned. This pitiful sight Peter talks about and want us to avoid. Believers must see themselves and their lives as preservatives of the God. Stay connected to Christ and you will be the salt of your world.

The fruit of light

Matthew 5:14-16, "You are the light of the world. A city that is set on a hill cannot be hidden. Nor do they light a lamp and put it under a basket, but on a lamp stand, and it gives light to all who are in the house. Let your light so shine before men, that they may see your good works and glorify your Father in heaven."

This chapter shows that Christians are not only to represent Christ in the world as salt but also as light. Light as we know is that which makes it possible to see everything around us as it is the opposite of darkness. Whenever light presents itself, darkness disappears. A practical example is a candle, a fire or lights produced by electricity. They produce light so you can find your way around a dark track or room. It illuminates and transforms the way we relate to things around us; it also represents a guiding force of that which is good. As Jesus said, "You are the light…"Christians also represent Christ (the light of the world) and therefore the nature of Christ which brings light into this world of darkness. Christians can do this only when they walk in the light. Ephesians 5:8 (NKJV) states, "For you were once darkness, but now you are light in the Lord. Walk as children of light."

As John wrote, Christians become the light of the world through Jesus Christ who is the true light of the world. In John 1:8-9 (NKJV) he states, "He was not that Light, but was sent to bear witness of that Light. That was the true Light which gives light to every man coming into the world." Again Jesus bears testimony of Himself saying, "…I am the light of the world. He who follows Me shall not walk in darkness, but have the light of life," in John 8:12 (NKJV). Again He said "I have come into the world as a light, so that no-one who believes in me should stay in darkness." John 12:46.

Jesus Christ is the light that came into the world. The Bible states that all those who believe in Him have passed from darkness to light. Similarly, it comes as a great relief for a person locked up in a dark room for a long time when the lights are turned on. Imagine a village that has never had access to electricity and the joy of the inhabitants on the first night the lights are turned on. I remember being personally present in a town in Ghana some years ago and witnessed extreme jubilation of the people there. Every person of the town was in jubilant mood because it was the first day the town was connected to the national electricity grid. This is the mood of the believer when Christ (the light of the world) is switched on and shines in their lives at which point the darkness disappears. In the same way, I have witnessed the faces of people who were under Satan's dominion, changed instantly when they received Christ into their lives.

This is the reason why believers are always in the spotlight and are always criticised, because we cannot hide as children of light. On the other hand, non-believers are hardly seen and criticised as they are in darkness. When you are in a room where there is light, when the door is open you can be seen by anyone outside standing in darkness. This happens as result of the light around you; however, you cannot see the person who is standing in the dark.

May I therefore remind all my fellow believers, to be extra careful of what you do? You have passed from darkness to light and so you are in the spotlight and can be easily seen by all. Writing to the Philippian church Paul expressed a sign of being united with Christ the Vine. He admonished believers to be shining stars in this crooked and depraved generation. He said, "Do everything without complaining or arguing, so that you may become blameless and pure, children of God without fault in a crooked and depraved generation, in which you shine like stars in the universe as you hold out the word of life in order that I may boast on the day of Christ that I did not run or labour for nothing." Philippians 2:14-16. I have to go against the opinion of those who take the battle into their own hands then say it's too difficult and challenging to live a godly life. Paul is saying that you must depend on God and he will give you the power to live a Christian or godly life. He also obligates you to do what is right and you will acquire the power to match His standard of living.

Writing to the Thessalonian church also, he said, "But you, brethren, are not in darkness, so that this Day should overtake you as a thief. You are all sons of light and sons of the day. We are not of the night nor of darkness. Therefore let us not sleep, as others do, but let us watch and be sober." 1 Thessalonians 5:4-6 (NKJV)

As Apostle Paul advises the Thessalonian church, so let me at this point give the same advice all my fellow believers. Exercise self-control at all times, understand that you cannot go to all places and do all the things. You should not watch everything because other people may be doing these things. I like the following proverb so I frequently use it, "Many animals eat the palm nuts but only the squirrel gets accused." "All animals will run; but often people will run away in fear and panic from a cow when it is running, saying that it is mad." Dignify yourself as child of light and live to reflect that for you are been watched by others.

Years ago, I met a man who happened to be a member of a witness movement of which I was the leader. This man tried to introduce me to a man he was walking with. When I stretched out my hand to shake the man's hand he looked at his friend's face with a look of surprise, then asked him "Oh! So are you Christian? I never knew you were." He indicated that that man's life outside the church was not right or in this context a light. You can imagine the shame that gripped the man at that moment.

Jesus states that you are the light of the world; we became the light of the world because we remain in Him according to all the scriptures above. He also said, "Let your light shine before men." This means that there is no other alternative for believers, but to be light wherever it is dark. By extension, this means you must promote good character everywhere as an example of God's light in an evil world. In concluding this topic, I want to ask you these questions: "Does what you say and what you do and who you are really confirm that you are connected to Jesus Christ - the Vine and the Light of this world?" the power to be light comes from Him so it is imperative that you stay connected to Him.

Fruits Of The Spirit

The fruit of the Spirit is also part of the fruits expected from believers, those who remain in Christ, those who are connected to Him. Writing to the Galatian church Paul proclaimed "But the fruit of the Spirit is love, joy, peace, patience, kindness, goodness, faithfulness, gentleness and self-control. Against such things, there is no law. Those who belong to Christ Jesus have crucified the sinful nature with its passions and desires. Since we live by the Spirit, let us keep in step with the Spirit. Let us not become conceited, provoking and envying each other." Galatians 5:22-26.

The fruit of the Spirit as listed in the quotation above by Paul are also some of the fruits borne by those who remain or stay connected to Christ. This means that when you are connected to Christ, as a believer, these fruits of the Spirit must be seen in you. A fruit can easily be identified as can a type of a tree. A proverb says, "A crab does not give birth to a bird." Everything brings out products of its kind. Those who have ever lived in a village or countryside where there is vegetation or forest can easily identify the kind of tree, e.g. a mango, orange or pear tree by its fruits scattered around it on the ground. Jesus said, "By their fruit you will recognise them. Do people pick grapes from thorn bushes, or figs from thistles? Likewise, every good tree bears good fruit, but a bad tree bears bad fruit. A good tree cannot bear bad fruit, and a bad tree cannot bear good fruit. Every tree that does not bear good fruit is cut down and thrown into the fire. Thus, by their fruit you will recognise them." Matthew 7:16-20. Therefore, if we say we are believers and have the Holy Spirit living in us, we must also produce the fruit of the Spirit that can be seen by others. I have already discussed some of these fruits earlier in the book, so I continue to highlight the other fruits. It is crucial that you should know about them and the nature of their importance.

The fruit of peace

Peace is an important factor of fruit bearing; it underpins the very nature of what is required to bear fruit for Christ. No one can bear the fruit of peace unless they stay connected to Him because He is the Prince of Peace (Isa 9:6). The peace of God is not based on the material things one has or the absence of war and fighting as defined by United Nations and other peace organisations. It is based on every aspect of God and is the most secure fortification irrespective of the situation around you. It brings understanding, the ability to forgive, freedom from conflict or disagreement among people or groups of people. It facilitates the ability to face the big challenges in your life, with the comfort that the Lord is in control and all is well.

Jesus said to his disciples: "Peace I leave with you, My peace I give to you; not as the world gives do I give to you. Let not your heart be troubled, neither let it be afraid." John 14:27 (NKJV). When you have his peace due to staying connected to him, it takes away any fear and anxiety irrespective of the situation. You can sleep with sound assurance, as you know that the Lord is in control. The confidence it gives means that you have no boundary because God and the Savior Jesus Christ have become the masters of your world. First, you have to let them take over your life by being connected to them. The psalmist David states, "I lay down and slept; I awoke, for the LORD sustained me. I will not be afraid of ten thousands of people who have set themselves against me all around," Psalms 3:5-6 (NKJV), these are the words of someone who has peace because of his relationship with the Lord.

The power to bear the fruit of peace is to stay connected to the Prince of Peace. Paul writing to the church in Philippi informs them to do away with anxiety when presenting their request to God. Through the power of prayer and thanksgiving, the peace of God will transcend all understanding and guard their hearts and minds through Christ Jesus.

Without peace, the Bible says no one can see God so it is better to seek to bear the fruit of peace.

The fruit of patience

One of the tests of fruit bearing is endurance and steadfastness; it represents the hallmark of a Christian who is committed to God's will The writer of the book of Hebrews states, "For you have need of endurance, so that after you have done the will of

God, you may receive the promise" Hebrews 10:36 (NKJV). Patience involves the ability to remain firm without moving and to withstand any storm of life. It also means you are able to maintain composure or to display self-restraint; this includes when you wait for God's promises and answers to your prayer. Equally, to be connected to Christ the Vine you must bear fruit of patience: which can mean the ability and willingness to allow others to express their opinions or to be able to tolerate others, their customs different from your own and also the reluctance to interfere with the freedom of thought or actions of others. Anyone with this fruit will be also reluctant to complain, find fault, or to say something is wrong, but would rather show tolerance and appreciate others. Lack of patience makes it difficult for one to have a good relationship with God and other people. It is a challenge for one to connect to Christ if these factors are missing; I will further address patience again in the book.

The fruit of kindness

Those who bear this fruit are equipped with an enormous amount of compassion. Every believer is expected to bear the fruit of kindness, the ability to understand the suffering of others and show a willingness to help them. They should also have empathy which is sharing of another's emotions, troubles, ability to understand another person as if what is happening to them is happening to you. Jesus Christ demonstrated this kind of fruit when he was here on earth. In Matthew 14:14 (NKJV) the Scripture says, "And when Jesus went out He saw a great multitude; and He was moved with compassion for them, and healed their sick." Again, He demonstrated the fruit of kindness when he wept at the news of the death of Lazarus even though he knew he will raise him from the dead. He wanted to prove to Martha and Mary the sisters of Lazarus that he shared their grief and anguish." John 11:33-35 says "When Jesus saw her weeping, and the Jews who had come along with her also weeping, he was deeply moved in spirit and troubled." "Where have you laid him?" he asked. "Come and see, Lord," they replied. Jesus wept."

This wonderful fruit enables those who bear them to be considerate as well as responsive to the thoughts and problems of others, as shown by the character of our Lord in the above Scripture. They are not selfish, never take advantage of the others but treat people with kindness and not hatred. On numerous occasions, Jesus Christ showed compassion to many and responded to their need, because he is the Vine. (Matthew 9:36; Matthew 14:14; Mark 1:41) Every bearer of this fruit also like Jesus always seeks the interest of others and always ready to help them. The Good Samaritan from the Scriptures is one example of a person who has this type of fruit, no wonder he received recommendation from Jesus for his act (Luke 10:25-37).

The fruit of goodness

Goodness is described as an act of being good or been righteous. No one can have this character unless he is connected to Jesus Christ through the Holy Spirit for it is the character of the kingdom of God. Paul states, "For the kingdom of God is not a matter of eating and drinking, but of righteousness, peace and joy in the Holy Spirit" Romans 14:17. One can only do what is right, or live to please God only when he is connected to Christ who is the road that leads to all righteousness. The fact of the matter is no one can demonstrate or bear any of the above good fruits without being connected to Christ the Vine; they are the fruits of the Holy

Spirit which bore out the testimony about the nature Christ's life. In other words, these fruits are the works, which the Holy Spirit accomplishes in man. Without the Holy Spirit, one is controlled by the flesh, which cannot do or bear any good thing even though one can have the desire to do so. Paul states, "For what I do is not the good I want to do; no, the evil I do not want to do—this I keep on doing. Now if I do what I do not want to do, it is no longer I who do it, but it is sin living in me that does it." Romans 7:19-20

The quotations above and below is prove of the fact that without the help of Christ the Vine no one (no branch) is able to do anything good for themselves or for others. This is the reason why many people are trying or have tried to do good things. The more they try the more failure have become part of their experience. I have seen and heard people who for many years tried to quit a habit they consider harmful for their health or their relationships. They quit it for many years, and then suddenly one-day they give up and reverted to their old habits.

Once I met a man, I knew who had been involved in several bad habits. He had stopped all those things and as a result looked well and calm. I was so impressed that I mentioned him in my sermon one day, unfortunately, after meeting again sometime later; I found that he has given up and he is back in the old habits. Even though I did not ask him why he has gone back, I am under the assumption he was trying to do it with his own strength. Another reason is that he did not give his life to Christ and to this day, he is still an unbeliever consumed by his soul destroying acts. There is something very important about this man's story; he wanted to bear good fruit.

However, this is only possible for those who are connected to Christ. Like many, the man could not achieve this with his own strength and that is why it did not work. Others are also having difficulty making peace and are totally devoid of patience. It is a challenge for them to love their own wife, husband and children comparing them more or less to the man on the street or neighbour. Everything becomes possible when one is truly connected to Christ and therefore is controlled by the Holy Spirit because as Paul said the life you lead is not you but Christ who lives in you.

Good Fruit And Bad Fruit

Something of equal importance to note; types of fruits in order to know which one you belong. Bearing good fruits glorifies God, silences the critics of our God and keeps believers connected to the Lord. On the other hand, bad fruits bring Him shame and disgrace.

Jesus told his disciples and indeed all believers that being able to live as salt and light, that is bearing the fruit of salt and light in this polluted and dark world brings glory to God and is proof that indeed we are sons and daughters of God. Matthew 13:16, He said "Let your light so shine before men, that they may see your good works and *glorify* your Father in heaven. John reiterates this in John 15:8 and supports the theme of this book. "By this My Father is *glorified*, that you bear much fruit; so you will be My disciples." He said this after he has said, "if you remain in me and my words remain in you, ask whatever you wish, and it will be given you". John 15:7 which to me means that if you stay connected to me and as a result receive answers to your prayers, that will make you happy and will bring glory to my Father. I want to make it clear to you that God is glorified when good things happen to his children not bad things.

I remember the testimony of a Moslem who gave his life to Christ in our church. He went from Ghana to London to find greener pastures without knowing anybody there. According to him when he was running out of money, he began going to the mosque intending to get help from his Moslem brothers. He did not get help there. One day on his usual outing to seek help he met a member of our church who brought him to me in church; immediately after telling me his story I was deeply moved and made an appeal for him and people responded with great love. They responded by giving money, clothes among other things. This is something we have done many times in our church to help people in need or in difficult times.

Some of these people we never see them again even though some made a promise to be part of us in serving God. We are not bothered as we are happy to help people for Jesus' sake whenever the need arises. This is why the Moslem man gave his life to Christ saying when he needed help Christians helped him. He noted that we did it even though we did not know him while those he regarded as brothers ignored him. I am left in no doubt, that such a good gesture brought glory to God or Jesus. It also points to the fact that we are really His disciples as he said in John 13:35.

On other hand, when believers fail to bear good fruit, they become unproductive and therefore bring reproach or shame to the Lord. This allows the enemies of God to blaspheme the name of the Lord instead of glorifying and attracting people to Him. This is what the prophet Nathan said when asked by God to rebuke David who sinned with Bathsheba and killed her husband Uriah. The prophet said: "However, because by this deed you have given great occasion to the enemies of the LORD to blaspheme, the child also who is born to you shall surely die." 2 Samuel 12:14 (NKJV)

In Romans 2:23-24 (NKJV) Paul states, "You who make your boast in the law, do you dishonor God through breaking the law? For, "the name of God is blasphemed among the Gentiles because of you," as it is written." Take into account that whenever God's name is blasphemed because of what we do or say a curse is brought on us but blessings are bestowed on us when what we do or say glorifies him.

What do I mean by good fruit glorifies God while the bad ones brings Him shame? It is glory to God when a person is transformed through the lives of others and as a result gives his or her life to Christ. People recognize the change and speak about how God is great to have transformed such a person. In most cases, others have given their lives to Christ because of the testimony of these individuals. On the other hand, those Christians who bear bad fruit are the ones that make it possible for people to speak against God and Christianity. The saddest situation is when the lives of these people prevent others from coming to Christ. In others words, when people say they will not come to Christ or church because of the way some Christians live their lives.

Paul again wrote to Timothy that Christian's slaves should treat their masters with respect so they will not have the opportunity to speak against the name of God. He said, "All who are under the yoke of slavery should consider their masters worthy of full respect, so that God's name and our teaching may not be slandered," 1 Timothy 6:1. There are many people in biblical days and in our time who may not be Christians but are aware that Christians must do good at all times and therefore expect them to behave in such a manner. Just as Paul wrote to Timothy to tell the Christians slaves of his time, I also urge you who are not slaves, but you are under authority, working to earn a living. I implore you to serve your master wholeheartedly as you would do for Christ. Seek to work earnestly to promote the interest of the business. This is a good fruit or character that brings glory to the Father. If you are a believer and you know that you are part to blame for the downfall of someone's business where you are working ask God for forgiveness, it is bad thing to do.

Daniel had the opportunity to work with unbelievers in an unbelieving nation of Babylon but the bible says he proved himself more efficient and capable than all the others through hard work and so earned great respect from the King who planned to set him over the whole kingdom. "Now Daniel so distinguished himself among the administrators and the satraps by his exceptional qualities that the king planned to set him over the whole kingdom," Daniel 6:3. I believe if we are to prove that we are connected to Christ the Vine, one of the ways to do so is to prove to our employers especially, the unbelieving ones through hard work. Do you not agree with me in saying Daniel's life was a great glory to God? I think you do!

In concluding this topic, I pray that you understand and accept all that I am telling you with a good heart. This way you can try your best to live a life pleasing God, which involves bearing good fruits, which will bring glory to Him. This is crucial if you want to share in the benefit of staying connected. Colossians 1:10-12 says, "And we pray this in order that you may live a life worthy of the Lord and may please him in every way: bearing fruit in every good work, growing in the knowledge of God, being strengthened with all power according to his glorious might so that you may have great endurance and patience, and joyfully giving thanks to the Father, who has qualified you to share in the inheritance of the saints in the kingdom of light."

Knowing The Word

Knowledge of the word or continued belief in the Good News helps you stay connected to Christ, the Vine and can help you to grow as a believer. Many people even though they have been Christians for many years are still babies unable to grow spiritually and into maturity. These spiritual babies are the ones who persistently judge things according to the flesh or feelings instead of God's word or Spirit. In the context of this book at this point, one can grow into maturity by staying connected to Christ through the knowledge of His word. It is important to note that through His word you will able to distinguish good from evil. You must do something if you want to grow in the Lord and have the ability to take in solid food. You must continue to believe the Good News, begin to study the word of God and put into practice what you learnt. Paul challenges the Philippian church when he said, "Whatever you have learned or received or heard from me, or seen in me put it into practice. And the God of peace will be with you," Philippians 4:9. For more details about how you can grow as a Christian read my book, **"Be Ye Transformed, the Steps to Spiritual Transformation".**

It is not good enough just to be born again or just being one of the branches for you can become an unproductive branch. Moses told the Israelites it is not enough just to have covenant with God. That means that just being an Israelite or a Christian is not good enough in our time. You must stay connected to Him and do His will, which means to do what He says to through the law or the word. "And Moses called all Israel, and said to them: "Hear, O Israel, the statutes and judgments which I speak in your hearing today, that you may learn them and be careful to observe them." Deuteronomy 5:1 (NKJV)

Growing in God's word is one of the greatest ways to stay connected to Him. Unfortunately, many Christians today are Christians only by name not by the knowledge in God's word. As a result, many are deceived. That is why Peter advised his readers "to lay aside everything and seek the word of God that is able to help them to grow into maturity."He said "As newborn babes, desire the pure milk of the word that you may grow thereby," 1 Peter 2:2 (NKJV). Many people have fallen by the wayside in their Christian life because they lacked the word, which is able to keep them firmly connected to Christ the Vine.

Helps believers to pray effectively – Praying in God's will.

As mentioned earlier when discussing the fruit of prayer, one of the major reasons why some of our prayers go unanswered is that we pray without scriptural backing. This means praying out of God's will, we pray using statements which are contrary to the word of God not knowing that He will only answer our prayer through his word or according to His will. The point I am trying to make here is that God will not answer our prayer because of our tears or the state of our condition; he will only answer when the prayer is based on his word as I said earlier on. Many Christians give into their emotions, cry a lot in their prayers, and leave faith behind. However, they need faith, which will connect their prayers to Christ to yield a result. The scriptures say in James 4:3, "You ask and do not receive, because you ask amiss, that you may spend it on your pleasures." 1 John 3:21-22 says, "Beloved, if our heart does not condemn us, we have confidence toward God. And whatever we ask we receive from Him, because we keep His commandments and do those things that are pleasing in His sight."

In 1 John 5:14, the apostle wrote "Now this is the confidence that we have in Him, that if we ask anything according to His will, He hears us." God's will is His word. To pray effectively in God's will is to pray according to what God has said in His word. He said He would never violate His covenant or alter anything that has come out of His mouth (Psalm 89:34). This means that anybody who prays according God's word is guaranteed to receive answers to his prayer as God is bound by His word. I will give you an example of the faithless prayer, which can work for an unbeliever but not for a believer. I have seen and heard many people who prayed this type of prayer when they were unbelievers and the Lord instantly heard and delivered them out of their problem. They said:

"Lord or Jesus if you are really there or exist and have power to save, please deliver or heal me as I have heard Christians say it. Please save, deliver or heal me and I will serve you the rest of my life."

However, I am totally against a believer using the same kind prayer which begins with "Lord if you are really there or exist". This usually happens out of sheer desperation and it is immature for a believer to pray this type of prayer. It is a prayer of unbelief, not part of God's will and is against his word. A believer should confidently thank God in every situation knowing that He exists and is able to do all things. This is the kind of prayer which is of God's will and He will have no alternative but to answer as it is done in faith. Note that you can only pray God's will or in line with God's word when you read the word and believe it because you cannot use God's word in your prayer when you don't know the word.

God's will

The reason why God will always answer prayers offered to Him according His will or His word is that he is bound by His will or His word.

Therefore, to pray God's will is to refer Him back to what He has said in His word. Below are sample quotations to prove my claim. He said to Isaiah, "Put Me in remembrance; Let us contend together; State your case, that you may be acquitted," Isaiah 43:26 (NKJV). What God is saying in this scripture is, "Tell me why I should answer your prayers?" Again, he said to Jeremiah in Jeremiah 1:12, "The LORD said to me, "You have seen correctly, for I am watching to see that my word is fulfilled," Jeremiah 1:12.

"God has exalted his word above his name, "I will worship toward Your holy temple, And praise Your name For Your lovingkindness and Your truth; For You have magnified Your word above all Your name," Psalms 138:2 (NKJV).

Helps the believer to grow in the knowledge of God and his power to lead a godly life

Many Christians are still struggling to lead a godly life while others are living a life being ignorant of whom God is and who they are in Christ Jesus. Many others also struggle to cope with some situations and find it difficult to stop habits, which are wrong and harmful to them. These habits tarnish the reputations, of some and represents a threatening health risk for others. This is all down to the fact that these people are out of touch with God through His word; they have stopped believing the Good News. Those who are in touch with the Lord through his word, all things will become possible for them. They will be able to cope with any situation, challenge and be able to stop any habit. Paul boldly declared that when he said; "I can do everything through him who gives me strength," Philippians 4:13.

Undoubtedly, the people in Peter's time were having the same problem we face today; his message is as relevant today as it was back then. He wrote, "Grace and peace be multiplied to you in the knowledge of God and of Jesus our Lord, as His divine power has given to us all things that pertain to life and godliness, through the knowledge of Him who called us by glory and virtue," 2 Peter 1:2-3 (NKJV). Holding the values of the Good News will help one to know that Jesus Christ in His divine power has provided everything we need to live a happy and godly life. It will also keep believers connected to Jesus Christ the Vine and will also prevent them from making so many mistakes - the kind that will later bring trouble. Philippians 2:13 stresses this fact when the writer says; "It is God who gives you the power to do His will." In verse 14, he says that because of this, we should do all things without complaining and arguing. The psalmist David also said: "How can a young man keep his way pure? By living according to your word," Psalms 119:9. Living a godly life as a young man in this evil world in a crooked and corrupt generation is not an easy thing to do. A young person today needs God's help and His Holy Spirit inspired word. I am always thankful to God who reached out His hands to save me in the prime of my teenage years. I can confess that there are so many life styles I have never tried I have no desire for them; admittedly the enemy persistently tried to attract me. Yet I have to acknowledge that as a youth I did some erroneous and disagreeable things.

In talking to some of the youths in and outside our Church (in London), I realize the pressure from peers, parents and the other social pressures of modern society. All of this makes it enormously difficult for young people to stay pure and follow

God's path. Suffice to say, the psalmist David says they can do so with the help of God's word - that is when they believe the Good News. If you are a young person reading this book, I want you to know that there is strength and support in the Word of God. I advise you speak to someone with experience in these matters who will give you the good and proper guidance. I can assure you that with Jesus and the power of his Spirit you can overcome any challenge in life. Paul said, "The sting of death *is* sin, and the strength of sin *is* the law. But thanks *be* to God, who gives us the victory through our Lord Jesus Christ," 1 Corinthians 15:56-57 (NKJV).

When I was young, I came under all sorts of pressure in my school days; people were saying it was impossible to live my life style. I refused to succumb to some of the pressures that were heaped on me; a tirade of abuse and insults (including name-calling) were hurled at me. There were those who even laughed at me because I refused to do certain things. They said that I would end up being a fool. Remarkably, none of what I heard or saw deterred or persuaded me to turn my back on my Christian values. I was determined because my knowledge of the Word informed me that it was a sin against God to do those things. I also knew through God's word, that there was a better life for me in the future as result of my commitment to Him. The word of God says that those who put their trust in God will never be put to shame. The result of my steadfastness is what you are now reading in this book. This is complimented and underpinned by my exalted position of a Pastor, a teacher of God's word and above all an author - to God be the glory. I remember when I was in technical school; some of my friends had planned to lock me in a room with a girl to see what would happen. It was something that made me laugh a lot when I heard of the plot. I remember saying to them locking me in a room with a girl means nothing, "you will come back to meet us in the same way you left us."

More quotations to support the fact that all things are possible to those who stay connected to God through his word.

"I have hidden your word in my heart that I might not sin against you," Psalms 119:11. Jesus Christ once told his listeners they are making mistakes because they lack the word and the power of God, Matthew 22:29. He also indicated as he prayed for his disciples that the word of God sanctifies, John 17:17 (NKJV).

2 Timothy 3:16-17 (NKJV), "All Scripture is given by inspiration of God, and is profitable for doctrine, for reproof, for correction, for instruction in righteousness. That the man of God may be complete, thoroughly equipped for every good work."

Those who stick to the Good News, read it regularly and practice it are more likely to know God's plan and purpose for His children. They will be able to lead a life, which helps them to distinguish between accurate and inaccurate teachings. Furthermore, they will also identify bogus information emanating from false teachers and prophets; they will be equipped with a sharpened sense of discernment. All the above scriptures reinforce the fact that your knowledge of God's word will assist you to improve your life for the better. This will also enable you to avoid the mistakes, which can affect you negatively for the rest of your life. Many people are suffering because of past mistakes because they lacked a connection with God. Whether you are a young or an adult reading this book I advise you to seek and live by the Word. The subtext of this is that you need to connect yourself to Jesus Christ the Vine; do it through the Word and you will reap the power or benefit here on earth and in the world to come.

Helps believers to remain firm in the Lord and in life

Many people these days are serial denominational grasshoppers, they move from church to church mostly due to lack of knowledge in the word of God. They think they could go to heaven because of the type of church they attend. Others think that it could help them to receive their miracle though God does not approve of the life they lead as they lack the Word. If you continue to believe the Good News, it will help you to remain firm in the Lord. This way the strong winds of deceit will not be able to blow the truth away from you. The Scripture warns believers to be very careful, otherwise they will be deceived. Romans 16:17-18 says, "I urge you, to watch out for those who cause divisions and put obstacles in your way that are contrary to the teaching you have learned. Keep away from them. For such people are not serving our Lord Jesus Christ, but their own appetites. By smooth talk and flattery they deceive the minds of naïve people." How would you know you are deceived? It is only when you are knowledgeable in God's word.

Paul's recommendation on the Berean Church: Acts 17:11, "These were more fair-minded than those in Thessalonica, in that they received the word with all readiness, and searched the Scriptures daily to find out whether these things were so."

We are only fooled, deceived by any doctrine because we do not study the word. Ephesians 4:14, "Then we will no longer be infants, tossed back and forth by the waves, and blown there by every wind of teaching and by the cunning and craftiness of men in their deceitful scheming."

1 Timothy 4:13-16, "Until I come, devote yourself to the public reading of scripture, to preaching and to teaching. Do not neglect your gift, which was giving to you through prophetic message when the body of elders laid hands on

you. Be diligent in these matters; give yourself wholly to them, so that everyone may see you your progress. Watch your life and doctrine closely. Persevere in them, because if you do you will save yourself and your hearers."

As it was in the days of the apostles so it is today, there are numerous false prophets and teachers out there. They have created a lot of confusion, division and placed obstacles in the way of people's growth. Without the correct knowledge of the Word, people have become a detrimental influence by infecting others with their poisonous information. These people can only be identified and possibly drawn away from these false prophets by being secure in the word of God.

Since I came to the Lord I have seen many people come and go; the word of God has sustained me until today. I have always taken it very seriously since the day Christ came into my life. I have faced many temptations, and been confronted with advice designed to distract me from Christ the Vine. They could have ruined my life but I was able to prevail over them because I went into battle with them using the word of

God. His grace became my shield and protector against the onslaughts of the enemy. I will never forget the training I had from my first presiding elder who always requested everyone should give a Bible quotation in Church. This placed added pressure on me to study the Word so that in such instances I will be prepared and not be stunned into silence as others were. This reminds me of something funny we used to do as young people in our church. My friends and I noticed that the old people in our Church would always give specific quotations whenever we were asked to give one in church, this was part of our service in those days. We would always rush to say ours first to deny the old people by using their quotations. They were crippled by their inability to quote new ones. It sounds funny now but if I asked you as a believer to give Bible quotations now how many can you give? I know there are many of you out there who may also be as crippled as those old people because you don't have any. If you are one of those people, I implore you to begin to study your Bible now. This way you will be able to offer a quotation if asked to use it as a weapon in times of difficulty or when evil threatens you.

The knowledge and practice of God's word brings hope

We live in a hopeless world, everything around us from the news to words from friends and neighbor are all filled with fear and dismay. The only hope we have in the world today is what the Lord offers through his word, our only hope is in God. "The things that were written before were written for our learning, that we through the patience and comfort of the Scriptures might have hope," Romans 15:4 (NKJV). Knowing God's word brings confidence because it will always produce what it says it will. As I stated earlier, there are just as many people unstable in life as in the church. Due to insecurity many believe that changing jobs and relationships would give them stability and happiness in life. Many Ghanaians go by the Akan proverb which is translated in English as "You will never have any better marriage if you are afraid to lose your husband or your wife" so these people don't make any effort to protect their marriage because they think they are not restricted to one place or person. I go against the elder's idea; I have always put it this way "Those who are afraid of losing their partners, are those who will always have better partners." Because these people are the kind of people who will always do all they can to protect their marriage because they live by the directives of God's word. It is for this reason that I cherish my own marriage and I do everything within my means to protect it.

You may be one of these people without hope and so changing locations, job and relationships assuming it would bring stability to your life. I want to use this opportunity to advise you that your knowledge and practice of God's word is much more powerful in transforming your life. It will also help you to stay connected to Christ. Before we proceed, I should remind you that we are dealing with some of the things which can help you or remain in Christ. In the context of this book it means to receive the power of staying connected to Him.

Dwelling In The House Of God

Sometimes I wonder why some believers stay away from church for such long periods, is something I find very difficult to do since giving my life to Christ. Dwelling in the house of God and being in fellowship with other believers will help you to stay connected to Him. David knew this and made it his priority to dwell in the house of God. He said: "One thing I have desired of the Lord, that will I seek: That I may dwell in the house of the Lord All the days of my life, to behold the beauty of the Lord, And to inquire in His temple. For in the time of trouble He shall hide me in His pavilion; In the secret place of His tabernacle He shall hide me; He shall set me high upon a rock," Psalms 27:4-5 (NKJV).

At this point, I ask you about your priorities: "Where are you spending your life, in Him or outside Him? How often do you desire to go to the house of God and how long do you stay there?" As a minister of God, I know how people react in church when they think the service is getting a bit longer: some people begin to look at their watches, some leave and some complain. Look at the psalmist David; he wanted to be in house of the Lord for the rest of his life, so that he would always be in connection with his maker. In so doing, he reckons he would be saved and well protected from his enemies. David boldly demonstrated and illustrated his confidence about 'being protected' through the power of staying connected to God. He declared, "Even though I walk through the valley of the shadow of death, I will fear no evil, for you are with me; your rod and your staff, they comfort me," Psalms 23:4. If you want safety and security in your life then you must stay connected to Christ and He will protect you. He will give you the same confidence that David had.

Why do you think that dwelling in the house of God meant so much to David? He explains it here: He said "I was glad when they said to me, Let us go into the house of the LORD?," Psalms 122:1 (NKJV). You can see that David's desire to serve God is powerful; he knew that staying connected would keep him dwelling in God's house. In this house, there is joy, peace, salvation, protection, comfort and encouragement from other believers. I am a positive example of this fact; part of the reason for my stability in God was due to the testimonies I heard from one of my early mentors, the late Apostle V. O. Boafo (details of these testimonies can be found in my book 'Be Ye Transformed').

The psalmist David's greatest desire was to be in the house of God all the days of his life. Sadly, this is not the case for many believers today. These days, people use the radio and television so they can listen to any preacher of their choice. This blunts their desire to be in the house of God. They detached themselves from being with other believers so that they cannot worship God in unity and strength. Those of us who have a desire to live in God's presence each day will be able to enjoy His relationship forever if we are connected and abide in him. How are you connected to him in terms of your church attendance, your bible reading and your prayer life? While I was writing this part of the book, the Holy Spirit told me some of you think it is not important to belong to any Church. You think that going to church does not make you Christian and you may have a point there.

However, you should also note that to be in the house of God connects you to Him at all times. If you are one of those people, then I have some advice for you; pray and ask the Holy Spirit to lead you into a Spirit filled and Bible believing church and it will help you. The writer of Hebrews advised his readers in the same manner, saying: "Not forsaking the assembling of ourselves together, as is the manner of some, but exhorting one another, and so much the more as you see the Day approaching," Hebrews 10:25 (NKJV). I believe it is quite clear that being in the house of God continuously is as good as all the other things that will help believers to stay connected to Christ. It also provides the many opportunities to enhance your fruit bearing. I will expand on this a later in the book. I want you to above all, continue to stay connected to Jesus by being regular in His house there you will be encouraged, strengthened and instructed in the word of God which you need more than anything in this world.

Productive And Unproductive Branches

What type of branch do you think you are? Are you productive or unproductive? Notice that both branches are connected to Christ. To those who think you are productive: What type of fruit are you bearing? Is your fruit sweet or sour? Note that you were saved to save others as John 15:16 says,"You did not choose Me, but I chose you and appointed you that you should , and that your fruit should remain, that whatever you ask the Father in My name He may give you." Are you doing your saving work? That is, are you bearing sweet fruit that attract others to Christ?

Also note that our fruits should last, remember to consider whether the fruits you bare are lasting. In terms of soul winning fruits, some of the reasons why some fruits do not last are:

The same people who brought them to Christ offends them

They do not set a good example to them

The souls (the fruits) are not properly followed up.

Is there **anything** or **anybody** in the kingdom of God that you can count as your fruit? What part do you play in God's kingdom? In terms of soul winning and fruit bearing, has your fruit lasted? If your answer is no, then I challenge you to check yourself to see if you are the reason why that is the case. If you find yourself in such a position, then it is perilously dangerous, because that is when you become a stumbling block. Jesus particularly warned his disciples to beware of becoming stumbling blocks to those who come to Him. He said: "But whoever causes one of these little ones who believe in Me to stumble, it would be better for him if a millstone were hung around his neck, and he were thrown into the sea," Mark 9:42 (NKJV).

You may be trying your best to do good or what is right, in your own way, but there's a way ordained by God for us to follow. Some people think that 'Christianity is all about your heart' and it does not require you to seek Christ's help. I have to say that these kinds of people do not have a commitment or relationship with Him. They could not be more wrong as Jesus clearly states, "I am the vine, you are the branches. He who abides in Me, and I in him, bears much fruit; for without Me you can do nothing," John 15:5 (NKJV). A branch cannot bare any fruit unless it is connected to the vine; the only way to bare fruit and to live a righteous life is to remain in Christ. You must stay firmly connected to the Vine you can only be productive through power or assistance from the Holy Spirit of Christ.

Do you really want to produce good fruit? Do you bring glory or shame to God? Are you bringing in or driving out, gathering or scattering fruits (souls)? Your answer to these questions lies in staying connected to Christ. The danger is that those who are unproductive or scatter the fruits of their harvest are in danger of being banished. Jesus states, "If anyone does not abide in Me, he is cast out as a branch and is withered; and they gather them and throw them into the fire, and they are burned." (John 15:2; 6). Those who are in the Lord but do not manifest any of the good fruits are unproductive branches. You may be a Christian but since you came to Christ you have not been able to bring any one to Christ. You may not have done anything or produced good fruit, which has brought glory to Christ and attracted people to him. This may due to your inability to witness or tell people about the Good News. Perhaps you are one of those people whose character causes people to turn away from Christ. I have met some people who have vowed never to go to church again, because of what so called Christians have done to them. What is worse is that some of the people who caused offense are the very people who brought them to Church some are even offended by some Church leaders.

Eternal Life

When you are connected, you have eternal life it is only Jesus Christ, the Son of God that offers eternal life. We live in a time known as the postmodern era where there are no absolutes. This so-called post modernity has issued a death sentence on the moral coding of God's word; it has declared war on the morality of right and wrong. The state has now become the arbitrator of right and wrong in society and in our homes. With secularism in the ascendancy, we are in grave danger of losing the authority to govern your home and our lives as decreed by the word of God. Secularism an offshoot of post modernity dictates that there is no central moral authority and every one can decide the efficacy of their decisions. Now you cannot tell anyone or even your child what is right or wrong; everyone has the right to decide the boundaries of their own morality and belief. Why am I saying these things? Because it is now a discriminatory and legal offence in our society today to proclaim that only Jesus Christ the Son of God offers eternal life. Paul states, "And without controversy great is the mystery of godliness: God was manifested in the flesh, Justified in the Spirit, Seen by angels, Preached among the Gentiles, Believed on in the world, Received up in glory," 1 Timothy 3:16 (NKJV).

Man lost the gift of eternal life in the Garden of Eden through the sin of Adam and Eve. It pleased God to restore eternal life again but only through one man the seed of the woman. He states, "And I will put enmity between you and the woman, and between your offspring and hers; he will crush your head, and you will strike his heel," Genesis 3:15.

Secularism again suggests that there is no absolute right or wrong in determining how something should be done; therefore, the right to worship God through anything or anybody has led to a mushroom of confusion and many new religions. Even some Christians are confused and now believe and share one of the greatest lie ever told by the Devil - that there is one God but there are many ways to worship him. The fact of the matter is that there is only one God and there is only one way to worship Him, through Jesus Christ as pointed out by Him and Paul respectively. Jesus answered his disciples when they asked him to show them the way to the Father, He said, "I am the way and the truth and the life. No-one comes to the Father except through me," John 14:6. Paul also wrote, "For there is one God and one mediator between God and men, the man Christ Jesus, who gave himself as a ransom for all men the testimony given in its proper time," 1 Timothy 2:5-6.

As a word of advice to those who were looking for Him because of what they will eat. He urges them to seek for the food, which the Son of Man, will give them that, is able to give them eternal life. "And when they found Him on the other side of the sea, they said to Him, "Rabbi, when did You come here?" Jesus answered them and said, "Most assuredly, I say to you, you seek Me, not because you saw the signs, but because you ate of the loaves and were filled. Do not labour for the food which perishes, but for the food which endures to everlasting life, which the Son of Man will give you, because God the Father has set His seal on Him," John 6:25-27 (NKJV).

The background of this quotation is that Jesus criticised the people who had followed him only for the physical and temporal benefits and not for the satisfying of their spiritual hunger i.e. the food that can give them eternal life. To relate this story to us today I would say many people think going to Church is all about prosperity, health, marriage or the needs of man. While others think the end of life is the end of grace, that is, there is no life after death and therefore do not worry about gaining eternal life; as a result they live their lives in a cavalier and destructive way.

Having, this type of idea some Ghanaians will say, "let us party, eat and drink for tomorrow we are dead and gone." No my friend, life does not end here on earth for when a man dies he is not dead forever. There is judgement after death and there is eternal life and eternal death, which is eternal separation from God. The writer of Hebrews says; "Just as man is destined to die once, and after that to face judgment, so Christ was sacrificed once to take away the sins of many people; and he will appear a second time, not to bear sin, but to bring salvation to those who are waiting for him," Hebrews 9:27-28. Therefore I implore you take the opportunity today and reach out for the saving grace of Christ the Vine to receive eternal life.

If any of the above supports your view, then Jesus is speaking directly to you. He is telling you, "Do not work for food that spoils, but for food that endures to eternal life, which the Son of Man will give you. On him God has placed his approval". He is the only one who offers eternal life; believe it or not, accept it or not, it is the truth. Friends, as you read this book I want you to get it clear today that there is life after death. Jesus proved this in a story in Luke 16:19-31 (the rich man and the poor beggar Lazarus). He also proved this by himself rising from death, as the angel said to the women who after the Sabbath, at dawn on the first day of the week, went to look for him at the tomb, "He is not here; he is risen" (Matthew 28:6). I have often wondered what would have happened if the woman had found Jesus' body in the tomb on that faithful Sunday morning. Where would the disciples be and where would Christianity be? What do you think? Your guess is as good as mine is.

Paul in 1 Corinthians 15:19-20 said, "If only for this life we have hope in Christ, we are to be pitted more than all men." He wrote this letter to the Church in Corinth when some of the people just as it is in our time today were finding it difficult to believe the resurrection of the dead (life after death) read Verse, 12-18. What Paul is saying here is that if it is true (as some Ghanaians will say) when a man dies he is dead forever then Christians are the most pitiful, they have wasted their time on earth serving God. Friends let me say this emphatically - life is not a football match where it is all over after the final whistle - there is a resurrection, which leads to eternal life or eternal death (total separation from God). Why not connect yourself to the one and only person who is able to give you eternal life. It is Jesus Christ the Vine. Having established the fact that life is not only here on earth but also after death let us go back to our theme at this point. I will do this in the context of 'Stay Connected to have eternal life.'

Eternal Life

There are many companies, offering life and types of insurances giving people numerous options, this way they can choose which one is suitable for them. I face the same dilemma whenever I renew my car insurance. However, God has through Jesus offered eternal life and it comes with a cast iron guarantee and approval for it. In fact, it is exclusive to Him only; when it comes to eternal life there is no other person you can choose from to give you this; there is no alternative as demonstratively shown by the quotations which follows. Jesus is the only connection who can connect anyone to eternal life offered by God. John 3:14-15, 'Just as Moses lifted up the snake in the desert, so the Son of Man must be lifted up, that everyone who believes in him may have eternal life.' (Vs 14 refers to Numbers 21:8-9)

John 6:27, "Do not work for food that spoils, but for food that endures to eternal life, which the son of man will give you. On him God has placed his approval."

John 10:27-28, 'My sheep listen to my voice; I know them, and they follow me I will give them eternal life.'

1 John 5:13, 'I write this to you who believe in the name of the Son of God so that you may be know that you have eternal life.'

Only to those who will believe in the name of Jesus Christ

As I said earlier on everyone is entitled to eternal life but to qualify you must be connected to Christ and believe in His name. John cautioned those who reject this good offer and choose another, that they would suffer the consequence. He said, "Whoever believes in the Son has eternal life, but whoever rejects the Son will not see life, for God's wrath remains on him," John 3:36.

The following quotation continues to support John's warning. "But now that you have been set free from sin and have become slaves to God, the benefit you reap leads to holiness, and the result is eternal life. For the wages of sin is death, but the gift of God is eternal life in Christ

Jesus our Lord," Romans 6:22-23. On this note and with due respect I am also warning those of other faiths other than Christianity (the true followers of Christ). The uncomfortable truth for you is that eternal life comes through only one man who is worthy to guarantee that. That man is, as stated in the Scriptures, "the seed of the woman,' (Genesis 3:15) "and his name is Jesus, the only begotten Son of God" (Galatians 4:4-5), "the only mediator between God and man," 1 Timothy 2:5-6.

Do you think life ends here on earth or in the grave? Do you share the view that God is one but you can worship Him through any means as some men think? On the other hand, do you worship Him for the sake of eternal life? Jesus is the only answer do you know him. Or like some you follow him only because of physical gain? Think about your answer.

I want to advice those who think life without Christ is better than life with Him that you are wrong. That is the worst possible option for you to consider, as it will be the greatest mistake of your life. Life in Christ is not only about being here on earth but also about the world to come; it is about eternal life, God's original plan for man. This is a life, which only Jesus can offer. Someone once asked a very sensible question: "Do Christians think that God is so wicked to let only Christians go to heaven while he allows the rest of the greater part of world's population (the unbelievers) to suffer and go to hell simply because they did not believe in Christ?" Emphatically, the answer is 'yes' because they refused to accept his offer of eternal life and Christ the Vine. Again, note this is not what Christians or anybody thinks but what God said through His word. The Bible says that Jesus is the only one God the Father; has granted His seal of approval. In all circumstances life without Christ is not going to be better as many think, it will be worse instead. You should never contemplate exercising such an option, as the consequences will be catastrophic.

Self-Control

The Bible says in 2 Timothy 3:3 that in the last days people will lose self-control, nevertheless God's expects everyone to exercise self-discipline, both believers and unbelievers alike. There are serious consequences for those who fail to do so as declared in the bible, "Like a city whose walls are broken down is a man who lacks self-control." Proverb 25:28

Self-control, the key word in the quotation above in the context of this part of the book means, discipline, will power: the ability to control your behaviour and impulses, which is your desire, your wish or your fancy. e.g. strongly wanting to have sexual relationship with somebody who is not your husband or wife or wanting to have something to satisfy your wish even though it may result you to sin or do something to harm yourself or someone else. If you fail to control your life you become vulnerable to any assault from the enemy

I must admit as human beings that it is not easy for us to use our own ability to exercise self-control over desires of our bodies. This is what I call the five senses of the flesh. Another concern for me is the fact that many people have suffered greatly for failing to exercise self-control. These are situations they faced and experienced; death, damaged relationships, ruined reputations and wasteful lives. Some people have died prematurely because they failed to control their lust for men, women or alcohol and smoking. Many have lost jobs and positions because of these habits while others have fallen into problems because they could not control their tongue. I have seen and heard many whose homes have been broken as result of this lack of self-control. I have also learned about men and women who have gotten divorced because they became influenced by the lust of the flesh. I will deal in much detail on self-control in my other book in future, entitled "Discipline Yourself." In spite of all of your frailties I assure you that reading this book will not only offer you eternal life but also will offer you the power to overcome any bad character as you stay connected to Christ the Vine.

The Scripture says, "The sting of death *is* sin, and the strength of sin is the law. But thanks be to God, who gives us the victory through our Lord Jesus Christ. Therefore, my beloved brethren, be steadfast, immovable, always abounding in the work of the Lord, knowing that your labor is not in vain in the Lord." 1 Corinthians 15:56-58 (NKJV)

Paul is a biblical example of those whose life was turned around for the better after they met Jesus Christ the vine. He testified to this fact when he defended himself against accusations that he led a rebellion; he was beaten and nearly killed in Jerusalem as a result. Paul told his accusers who he was and what he used to be but was now saved by Christ Jesus. See Acts Chapter 21 - 22 and his letter to the Church in Galatians 1:11-16.

Like Paul, many people have been delivered and set free from many kinds of addictions. These include the repairing of damaged relationships and the restoration of soiled reputations. Many who have been rejected and neglected by families and societies have been welcomed back and regained their respect. This is more so now because they received Christ, the Vine and life-changer into their hearts. Jesus is the only man who has ever lived who is able, and so has changed the lives of many demon possessed, drunkards, and murderers, adulterers, fornicators and idolaters. Contrary to the teachings of Jesus and his followers I can also say that in many religions the teachings of their leaders has changed many lives from better to worse. Jesus is like a tree, which is bountiful when all of its branches blossom and bear many fruit.

Similarly, he wants all believers and those who are connected to Him to bear plenty fruit. Not only did Jesus offer power to overcome sin, evil desires and the flesh but also you will be an example of a liberated life deeply immersed in Him. The power, which emanates from this will attract and draw those seeking freedom of the same nature. You may criticise Paul for persecuting the Church of God and trying to get rid of it. But what you may not know is that perhaps your actions and the way you are leading your life is not acceptable and is not helping you. And in this context you are also destroying the peace and reputation of yourself and your family. You may even consider death as the best solution to your situation, but there is a better option for you. By whatever means you have got hold of this book, I want you to know that it is not by chance or by accident as many may sometimes put it. It is by divine appointment that your hour of deliverance has come. Jesus has come to rescue you from the mess in which you may find yourself. Similar to Paul your life will be changed for the better and you will be able to testify about the goodness of God to others.

A woman came to me one day and told me how she had considered ending her life because she had had enough of this world. She thought her life was worthless and miserable so being dead was the best solution; but I told her ending your life would not solve her problem but rather worsen it. I told her that taking her life is an unforgivable sin and that she would go to hell to suffer eternally. Instead of choosing death, I advised her to stay connected to Christ and He will help her overcome any problem she was going through. Later the lady, told me what I told her had saved her life and in fact gradually she became a happy woman and is now getting on with her life.

I have heard numerous testimonies about people whose lives have been transformed as a result of coming in contact with Jesus Christ. Some of these individuals have been able to refrain from habits and other addictions they suffered for many years. I remember the testimony of a man who was heavily addicted to smoking so that he could not go to the toilet in the morning unless he had a smoke – such was the psychological grip. Another man said he needed a woman on a daily basis, and could not go to bed without one. I remember the shock I had when a woman also told me the number of men she has slept with; she treated sex as her hobby just for fun. However, I would describe that as the work of the Devil who wanted to destroy her. However, glory be to God, these individuals have been set free from all these deviant behaviours since coming in contact with the master Jesus Christ. Another woman said she could not say no to a man when proposed to because she thinks a refusal will be humiliating to him. I have also known of others who were without Christ, yet used their human effort to stop some of these habits for many years. The difference is that after many years of abstinence, suddenly they return to the old life style. I was not surprised as I believe that no one can successfully fight these desires of the flesh with the flesh. Anyone facing these challenges will need assistance from the One who has power over all these things. Those liberated from these things are free forever as long as they stay connected to Christ. "So if the Son sets you free, you will be free indeed." John 8:36

When I was young, my mother used to say one day while she is having a meal, my dead body will be brought to her. Why do you think a lovely mother would like say this? Back then, I was very temperamental and as a result got into many fights. Unfortunately, for me nosebleeds were a big problem; during my fights, blood would run from my nose and down my shirt. When my mother or anybody saw me in such condition, they panicked. I remember the phrase, which was used for me in those times; people used to say, "He's been beaten to the point where blood is pouring from his nose". Thank God, when I met Jesus: he saved me, gave me eternal life, took away my quick temper and that fighting spirit. In the process, it also set my mother free from the fear of someone beating me to death; my mother got the peace she wanted. Hallelujah!

If you have been rejected due to addiction or any kind of negative characteristic, you have lost control of your life. It would also suggest that you have come to the end of the road. If you have become a burden for your parents, wife or husband and even your children I have good news for you. Come to Jesus and He will save you. Stay connected to Him and you will experience the joy of the power of being connected to Him. He will fix your broken life. There is a woman's testimony that I heard years ago in Ghana. She said one of the worst things she did was to ask her boyfriend to go to Nigeria to seek greener pastures; she told her boyfriend that it would be a good opportunity to improve their lives. Unfortunately, after some time she was told that he had been brought back to Ghana with serious and life threatening sickness. He was admitted to hospital and requested that she visit him, angrily she refused to go, saying she expected him to bring back money and other material things to make their lives better, instead he brought back sickness. Because of his illness, she decided to end their relationship and did not visit him at the hospital.

Thank God, after years of a disorderly life in the world, He is the only one who gives us victory over sin this lady came on the platform at a crusade organized by the witness movement and testified about the saving grace of Jesus Christ. She was really joyful and giving God the glory. The lady ended her testimony by saying that not only did Jesus save her, but he had also changed her name. People now call her 'A lady Pastor or A lady Minister.' it is with a little or a lot. Notice again that no one can change himself or herself by his own effort; God does the changing through your faith in his Son Jesus Christ. Therefore, stay connected to Him and he will transform your life for the better. What a good God we have; praise His name! You can also be like these individuals, your life will be transformed and you will be given a new name. Come to Jesus, stay connected to Him and you will experience life to its fullest. He will enable you to exercise self-control over your life. It can be achieved do not say, "I can't" for as stated by Paul in 1 Corinthians 15:56-57. He said

"But thanks be to God! He gives us the victory through our Lord Jesus Christ". I want you to rest assure and let it settle in your mind that as you stay connected to Jesus Christ the Vine through Him you will be able to overcome any habit or sin for He has already won the victory for you.

Focus On Christ

Focusing on Christ is one of the many ways of remaining in Christ and staying connected to Him. The Bible states that the disciples were first called Christians in Antioch (Acts 11:26) because others saw that their works reflected that of Jesus. They bore His mark and stayed connected to Him, even when He has ascended to his father. This means that Christianity should be Christ focused. Believers should be focus on Christ alone. Christianity is centered on Christ and its practice should be the essence of how he lived. Unfortunately, many people call themselves Christians but have no focus on Christ. They have no connection to Him and therefore get no direction from Him. This is the cause of so much desperation and confusion amongst most believers today.

Some of us are so confused and even doubt the truth of our God. It is a mirror of Gideon's decision as illustrated in Judges 6:12-13, 'When the angel of the Lord appeared to Gideon, he said, "The Lord is with you, mighty warrior." "But sir," Gideon replied, "if the Lord is with us, why has all this happened to us? Where are all his wonders that our fathers told us about when they said, 'Did not the Lord bring us up out of Egypt?' But now the Lord has abandoned us and put us into the hand of Midian."

I was talking with a woman once who told me that she had lost interest in her relationship with God because she has been overwhelmed with problems. The woman thought that God had abandoned her because it seemed she had come to the end of the road. Again, I have to give God the glory because after advising her she agreed to reconnect herself to the Lord, which she did. I have noticed a very worrying trend, which has given me cause for concern. People of other religious faith practice their faith with much more fervor than most Christians do today. Christ would have been more elevated and glorified and many unbelievers would have come to know Him, if Christians were earnestly focused on the Master. I will give you a good example of this: there is a Mosque in the same vicinity where we meet for our services and when it is time for the Moslems to go to Mosque they turn up in their numbers – men, women and even children. Their vast numbers usually cause a lot of traffic jam in the area. Sadly, on some days I go through the traffic to reach our church meeting place, only to find how low the numbers are. This is despite hosting three different church services in the building. It is not as though nothing is happening and this leads me to question myself about what the Christians are really doing.

The writer of Hebrews 12:1-3 advises his readers and indeed all believers who are being persecuted because of their faith to take consolation in Jesus Christ. He is the beginning and the end of their belief in God. "Therefore, since we are surrounded by such a great cloud of witnesses, let us throw off everything that hinders and the sin that so easily entangles, and let us run with perseverance the race marked out for us". "Let us fix our eyes on Jesus, the author and protector of our faith who for the joy set before him endured the cross, scorning its shame, and sat down at the right hand of the throne of God. Consider him who endured such opposition from sinful men, so that you will not grow weary and lose heart."

The following points arise from the quotations as deduced by me:

1. Christian life is a race in this context.
2. This race is set before a crowd of many witnesses, past believers (some of these witnesses or faithful men are listed in chapter 11) and from whom they can take encouragement. These are people who ran the same race and won through faith.
3. In this race there are many oppositions; terrible things, bad people and sins which can often distract your attention from Jesus. He is the only one who is able to help them to win the race.
4. The method of winning the race is to set Christ before us, focus on Him and make Him our example.
5. They should know that in spite of how tough the going may be there is no permanent situation; with Christ there is always victory and happiness at the end of the tunnel.
6. Using Jesus as an example, the writer said "for the joy set before Him" knowing his

position awaits Him at the right hand of the throne of God His father; he endured the cross while scorning its shame.

7. To win the race the writer says believers need patience and endurance.

8. I also believe that looking unto Jesus is that He provides the answer. He is not only the reason for our faith; He is also the image (example) of our faith which we should focus on, he is a true example of the fact that victory is not easily won. Through hard work and determination, Jesus suffered greatly at the hands of the people he later saved. Then He was exalted to the right hand of the throne of God.

Similarly, as believers we must not be weary or lose heart in our effort to serve God and to live a godly life. We must also know that as it was in the days of the Bible so it is now. Today, Christians still struggle and suffer in many areas of their lives because of their faith. They face problems everyday and everywhere. As a reader of this book, I have this word of encouragement for you; you are not the first person to have a bad experience and will not be the last. There are testimonies of some faithful men of the past, which will encourage you to carry on; they are available for you and detail all that it takes to succeed. According to the aforementioned Scripture above, in order to be able to survive you must focus on Christ. Here are some of the examples of Jesus' life:

1. He suffered at the hands of those He created
2. He went to the cross despite the shame. He died to save mankind
3. He did so because of the joy set before him
4. That is, sitting at the right hand of God the Father
5. Making intercession for his people (Rom 8:34)

This means that no matter what lies ahead of focusing on Christ Jesus will give you the strength, courage and hope to face every situation in life.

Some Of The Benefits For Those Who Focus On Him

As I said earlier on, many people in the world today including Christians question the sincerity of God and his loving care. When they see so many wars, hatred and misery, disease, and death and hunger their faith in God is severely shaken. Their ignorance compounds the situation as they lack the knowledge to understand such things. They often ponder and ask, "If He does care why are all these things happening? Why can't He prevent them?" To complicate matters some teachers and preachers teach that God is the cause of all that is happening - both good and evil.

I am here to proclaim that God still cares though he allows all things to happen he is not the cause of everything except the good things as James stated, "Every good gift and every perfect gift is from above, and comes down from the Father of lights, with whom there is no variation or shadow of turning," James 1:17 (NJKV) The good news about this situation is that God protects and provides for His children at all times. Focus on Christ, look to Him as the source of your living and concentrate on Him no matter what you do. Do not lose sight of Him as this connects you to Him and to God the Gardener who will take care of you at all times. If you follow these instructions, your security and provision is assured.

Security

One of the key benefits of focusing on Christ the Vine is God's protection of His children from the enemy or the Devil. Many people may not agree with me but the Scripture reinforces my belief that the Devil is always waging war against people in order to distract them from Christ the Vine. This war is fought on two fronts - the spiritual and the physical. I want to emphasize that no matter which type of the war you are involved in God will always protect you from any onslaught from the evil one. However, you have to keep your eyes on Him, remain in Him and stay connected to Him.

Spiritual Warfare

There is a war being waged against people both unbelievers and believers in the spirit. It is a war to gain the soul or spirit of a person not for material things. In this type of warfare, the Devil in his mission to destroy souls uses demons or evil spirits who cruelly and maliciously cause havoc to his victims. He inflicts sicknesses and all sort of problems in the lives of people, because the Devil has no mercy for anyone, he is very wicked.

The Bible says he only comes to steal, to kill and to destroy (John 10:10). One of the Devil's unmerciful acts is found in Mark 9:17-18 where it states Jesus healed a Demon possessed man. This is how the story unfolds: "A man in the crowd answered, "Teacher, I brought you my son, who is possessed by a spirit that has robbed him of speech. Whenever it seizes him, it throws him to the ground. He foams at the mouth, gnashes his teeth and becomes rigid. I asked your disciples to drive out the spirit, but they could not."

Man can only survive in this spiritual warfare if he also resists or fights the Devil in the spirit. This means when man is assisted by a superior spiritual means that is through the power of God, it is not the kind of war that can be fought using natural means like guns, swords or bombs; it takes spiritual means. Paul gave a fitting example when he wrote a letter to the Corinthian church. He defended his ministry against his enemies who were trying to distract him from his call. They wanted to divert him away from what connected him to Christ – the one who has called him. Unsurprisingly, some of the Corinthian church members continued to slander, insult and disrespect him. His enemies said he was extremely bold in his letters but his authority diminished in person. Paul described the spiritual might and the authority, which robustly armed him against all enemies. He said, "For though we live in the world, we do not wage war as the world does. The weapons we fight with are not the weapons of the world. On the contrary, they have divine power to demolish strongholds. We demolish arguments and every pretension that sets itself up against the knowledge of God, and we take captive every thought to make it obedient to Christ," 2 Corinthians 10:3-5

Here Paul is saying that every believer should emulate his approach; we do not respond to our enemies in the same way as the world does to resolve things. On the contrary, we should do them in the way that Christ did. We should use God's might through the Spirit to pull down every stronghold; in other words, the plans of the Devil. You must always keep your eyes on Him if you want to do things His way. Paul told the Ephesian church that Jesus Christ the Vine is the only armour; believers need to fight the Devil in order to overcome him and be able to stand in these evil days. (Read Ephesians 6:10-18 for more details). Never allow anyone or anything to influence you to take your eyes off Jesus. Stay connected to Him at all times for he is well able to take care of whatever spiritual problem you will face in life. He came to suffer so that he will be able to help those who will suffer as the writer of Hebrew said in Hebrews 2:14-15. "Since the children have flesh and blood, he too shared in their humanity so that by his death he might destroy him who holds the power of death—that is, the devil and free those who all their lives were held in slavery by their fear of death."

This is similar to when parents suffer in life for the sake of their children to lay a good foundation for them; so their children would not have to go through the difficulties and challenges they endured. In the same way you must take advantage of what Christ has done for mankind by keeping your eyes on him. Note that Christ is God and man so he knows your feelings as a human. He knows what it means to be sad and to be happy. The Bible illustrates his nature as man when he wept after he learnt of the death of Martha's and

Mary's brother Lazarus, John 11:35. Here Christ identifies with their sorrow and demonstrates that He cares for them. He shares his grief with the sisters even though He knew He was going to raise Lazarus from the dead, John 11:38-44

He always does things, which surpass the expectations of those whose eyes are fixed on Him. This is because He has the power to do all things at anytime as stated in Scriptures, "Now to Him who is able to do exceedingly abundantly above all that we ask or think, according to the power that works in us, to Him be glory in the church by Christ Jesus to all generations, forever and ever." Amen. Ephesians 3:20-21 (NKJV)

Again the Scripture says "You are of God, little children, and have overcome them, because He who is in you is greater than he who is in the world" 1 John 4:4 (NKJV)

Whatever the Devil promises you will be false as he is a liar and is limited in what he can do. Suffice to say, he uses cunning and deceitful methods; through some unexpected and unthinkable channels which makes it difficult to detect that he is at work. It takes the Spirit of God or Christ to uncover his hidden evil ploys; he uses friends, loved ones and your emotions as part of his sinister operation. Once the Devil tried to influence Peter to persuade Christ not to go to Jerusalem where he was going to die. However, Jesus sensed his presence and made Peter aware that it was Satan - so He rebuked him. "From that time on, Jesus began to explain to his disciples that he must go to Jerusalem and suffer many things at the hands of the elders, chief priests and teachers of the law, and that he must be killed and on the third day be raised to life. Peter took him aside and began to rebuke him. "Never, Lord!" he said. "This shall never happen to you!" Jesus turned and said to Peter, "Get behind me, Satan! You are a stumbling-block to me; you do not have in mind the things of God, but the things of men." Matthew 16:21-23 (ANIV)

There are many who may not even want to hear or discuss anything about the Devil and evil spirits because they do not even believe in their existence. There are also those who either underestimate or overestimate the Devil's powers. The third group are those who fear the Devil and his work even more than God's work. Whatever you think of the

Devil, he and his destructive deeds are real as I will demonstrate through a few testimonies. These will highlight my encounter with the powers of darkness and prove my assertion.

When I was a teenager, I lived with my father in a town in the Eastern Region of Ghana. One night around 2 a.m. in the morning I awoke, left my cousin sleeping and went outside to the front of the room to urinate. The moon was so bright, that it was as clear as day, outside, In African village life, it is very quiet, scary and dangerous at that hour, so it takes courage to come out in these times. As I urinated what appeared to be a hawk landed on the corner of next building where I was standing. In a flash, the bird disappeared turning into a woman who was also in the posture of urinating. Fear and panic gripped me so I hurriedly rushed inside and tried to lock the big door; I had to stand on a stool in order to do this. Suddenly, there was a big bang, and something hit the door with such force that I was hurled on to my sleeping mat. My cousin was awoken by this powerful commotion; he was in a daze and had no idea of what was happening. An old woman with a walking stick entered the room and embarrassingly slapped me three times on my buttocks. She said, "You bad boy! What are you doing out at this time of the night?" When the old woman left, I was petrified with anxiety and cold with terror. It is to be noted, that at the time I was a teenager not even born again; I was defenseless unable to call on the name of Jesus Christ as I would have done today. It is the only name that the Devil fears, the sound of it and makes him uncomfortable. However, I am grateful to God who knew me, protected me, and delivered me from that dreadful experience. The aftermath of that encounter was that I began to experience serious waist pains, but again when I came to know Christ, He healed me.

Before this incident, my father was a herbal doctor in that same town and people came to him for medicines to cure their sicknesses. Convulsion was one of the most widespread illnesses he treated, which was mostly suffered by children. One day a child who was convulsing was brought to my father. As was his custom, he went to the bush to bring the leaves he used to cure the attack. I was his trainee and had to administer first aid to the child;

a concoction of herbs in a pot left in the corner of our room. When my task was complete, my father would then come to do the rest of the job. However, on this occasion something different happened; he had to go three times to collect leaves for the portion. When the people left, I asked him why he had had to go three times on this occasion. He told me that the first time when he came back with the leaves and saw the faces of those with the child, the leaves in his hand became slippery like okro - or okra. My dad added that this made it difficult to squeeze water from the leaves, so on the third time he decided not to look at their faces. That was how he was able to get something out of the leaves to use. A few days later my dad told me someone from among the group who brought the child gave him a stern warning about his efforts to save the lives of children from convulsion attack. According to my father that person threatened him further; she chillingly warned that she and her group will turn against him if he did not stop saving these children's lives, informing him that he was putting his own children's life at risk. I have often wondered if the dreadful experience of that night had anything to do with this warning that was given to my father.

Anyway, I thank God I am still alive as many have had such experiences and did not survive, either through fear or other challenges.

In another experience in my early years as a believer, I had a dream one night that I went out in the town, as I was walking, I saw a long queue of many people; I was able to identify a lady who had come to know Christ through me. I got hold of her and dragged her from the queue and to my surprise; this action infuriated the people in the queue. They rushed towards me with sticks and clubs, shouting, "You are the one who wanted to take from us someone of our group." Everyone wanted to hit me with what they had in their hand, but by the grace of God none of them succeeded in hitting me. Praise and glory to God! When they rushed towards me, I also miraculously found a stick similar to the ones they were swinging at me. I held it up against them, so this thwarted their plans. Every time I threw my stick, I shouted Jesus' name and all those around me fell down. I woke up the next morning very terrified so I decided to fast that day.

Later that afternoon a woman came to me and said that she wanted me to come to her home and pray for her sick sister. I prayed for the sick and afflicted routinely at the time. I followed the woman to her house, to my surprise, I was led to the bathroom where I found one of her sisters lying unconscious on the floor. I noticed her body was wet; perhaps water was poured on her to revive her. As soon as this woman saw me she raised up her head, looked me in the eye and said: "Young man forgive me for I have sinned." I was shocked at her statement and asked her why. She replied, "I was fighting with a very handsome young man who hit me with a stick and I fell down and am not able to stand or walk since." The woman continually asked me to pray to my God so she would be forgiven and healed. I will never forget how I trembled as my stomach rumbled. I raised my hand and said one of the shortest and most powerful prayers I have ever done, "Lord if this had not happened your glory may not have been revealed, you have revealed this not only in my dream but physically too, please Lord heal this woman in Jesus name, Amen." I left there and went to my home, sometime later I went back to see how she was doing she was no longer in the bathroom but lying in her bedroom. When she saw me, she said, "Young man I thank you so much for your God has heard your prayer and healed me. You should share this testimony where ever you preach the word of God, Praise God." This is the reason why I am sharing this with you today. I remember after she said this, one of her sisters tried to be clever and reminded me that it did not mean I should make fun of her sister – "Even when you are playing with your friends." Friends I can share more stories about what I have seen not one thing I have heard or seen proves the Devil is real.

In spite of all what I have said about the Devil and his works and my personal testimonies or encounters, my main message is that Jesus has defeated the Devil and is well able to free those whose eyes are on Him. He secured His victory over the Devil when he was on the cross and stated, "It's finished." Paul had a fitting description to this when he said, "When you were dead in your sins and in the uncircumcision of your sinful nature, God made you alive with Christ. He forgave us all our sins, having cancelled the written code, with its regulations, that was against us and that stood opposed to us; he took it away, nailing it to the cross. And having disarmed the powers and authorities, he made a public spectacle of them, triumphing over them by the cross" Colossians 2:13-15

Physical warfare

This is the fight that challenges mankind where the Devil and the forces of darkness use others to wage war against other people, this fight relates to the physical rather than the spiritual. In this physical fight, God or Jesus (the Vine) always fights for those whose eyes are on Him. In one such fight King Jehoshaphat with God defeated the nations of Ammon, Moab and Mount Seir because his eyes were on God.

Jehoshaphat Focused On God

Jehoshaphat and his men worshiped God and told Him of their dependence on Him and the Lord promised them victory. You can achieve the same thing if you will worship Him and show your dependence on Him in times of trouble; this would also indicate that your eyes are on Him. 2

Chronicles 20:10-12, "But now here are men from Ammon, Moab and Mount Seir, whose territory you would not allow Israel to invade when they came from Egypt; so they turned away from them and did not destroy them. See how they are repaying us by coming to drive us out of the possession you gave us as an inheritance. O our God, will you not judge them? For we have no power to face this vast army that is attacking us. We do not know what to do, but our eyes are upon you."

The above story, beginning from the first verse tells of an interesting victory won by King Jehoshaphat and Israel. It also begs the question 'who do you turn to when the going gets tough particularly if you are a believer and the enemy seems to have won the victory over you.' How about when your loved one or someone you have helped turns against you? Just like Jehoshaphat, you do not know what to do? Always remember that God is eternally faithful and helpful to those whose eyes are on Him. The prophet Nahum said "The LORD is good, a refuge in times of trouble. He cares for those who trust in him," Nahum 1:7

The Lord's Promise of victory for Jehoshaphat and Israel

(2 Chronicles 20:14-17)

After the King and his people indicated to the Lord they were depending on Him, the Lord came down to speak to his people by giving the assurance and comfort that He will fight for them.

The Scripture says, 'Then the Spirit of the LORD came upon Jahaziel son of Zechariah, the son of Benaiah, the son of Jeiel, the son of Mattaniah, a Levite and descendant of Asaph, as he stood in the assembly. He said: "Listen, King Jehoshaphat and all who live in Judah and Jerusalem! This is what the LORD says to you: 'Do not be afraid or discouraged because of this vast army. For the battle is not yours, but God's. Tomorrow march down against them. They will be climbing up by the Pass of Ziz, and you will find them at the end of the gorge in the Desert of Jeruel. You will not have to fight this battle. Take up your positions; stand firm and see the deliverance the LORD will give you, O Judah and Jerusalem. Do not be afraid; do not be discouraged. Go out to face them tomorrow, and the LORD will be with you."

The Lord won the victory for his people - 2 Chronicles 20:22-25

God proved his faithfulness by always fulfilling his promise as He came to fight for His people. The Bible states, "As they began to sing and praise, the LORD set ambushes against the men of Ammon and Moab and Mount Seir who were invading Judah, and they were defeated. The men of Ammon and Moab rose up against the men from Mount Seir to destroy and annihilate them. After they finished slaughtering the men from Seir, they helped to destroy one another. When the men of Judah came to the place that overlooks the desert and looked towards the vast army, they saw only dead bodies lying on the ground; no-one had escaped."

I surely believe that the Lord promised and won victory for Israel because their eyes stayed on him. They relied on him, looked to him, depended on him; they gave Him the chance to fight for them. If you will allow Him, He will do the same for you. He cares more than any parent does, and is closer than any friend is. The Lord is able and will go with you where no one else can He is qualified and able to win every fight for you for He has never lost a fight.

This interesting story above raises the question again "Who do you turn to in times of trouble?" What do you focus on or whom do you rely on in the race of life set before you? Remember that as a believer you cannot do anything without Him. Many believers struggle in the fight against sin, habits and the enemy because God is not in the fight. Unwisely, they want to rely on their own strength. Consequently, many are running away from the power of darkness rather than have the enemy running away from them. This is as result of their eyes not being on Him. There are those who think they can use their money, husband or wife, jobs or qualifications to fight battles. Unfortunately, for them it does not work that way, God does not help those who think they can do it on their own or those who will only partially involve him. Jehoshaphat's declaration proves that he relied on God totally; therefore, the Lord brought the victory for his people by fighting for them. 2 Chronicles 20: 12, "O our God, will you not judge them? For we have no power to face this vast army that is attacking us. We do not know what to do, but our eyes are upon you". When you focus on God or Christ, victory is always assured, I have mentioned to people many times that such declarations leaves God with no alternative but to rush to your rescue for His own glory.

The Lord will do the same for you if your eyes are on Him, he will fight your battle. This always reminds me of advice my wife always gives to people who seek her counsel in times of persecution or troubles. She says, "If you know how to fight your fight the Lord will not fight for you." In other words, she always advises people to place whatever situation they face into God's hands. He will resolve it for them and it will be to His glory. Those who have heeded her advice and focused on Christ have always seen victory in their lives.

In Psalms 16:8, (NKJV) David states, "I have set the Lord always before me; because He is at my right hand I shall not be moved." God always protects those whose eyes are on Him, going before His children to fight on their behalf. When your eyes are on Him, you are connected to Him and therefore safe in His hands. In his words, the psalmist states that to stay connected to God, believers must remain in Him. This comes by permanently dwelling and remaining in Him. This means that you and He must become totally intertwined so you are protected and secure. The psalmist said, "He who dwells in the secret place of the Most High Shall abide under the shadow of the Almighty." Psalm 91:1 NKJV. He also reminds those who abide in Him that he will deliver them from the trap of evil. He will cover them with His protective feathers. In this situation they don't need to be afraid of the Devil's unrelenting round the clock attack on them. The Psalmist states that the Devil often comes in different disguises, but with a thousand (soldiers) on your side and ten thousand on the other side still it shall not come near you. If you are connected to God and your eyes are on him then you will see the end of the wicked.

Those who keep their eyes on God are always safe because the Lord has commanded His angels to keep them. In the last two verses 15 - 16 he states he will answer when they (those whose eyes are on him) call on Him in times of trouble. He also said the Lord would grant long life and salvation to all who take refuge in Him. (Psalm 91:1-16) What better comfort and the promise of peace could any parent give to their children? - It must be a sure promise that has power to produce whatever is requested.

Hezekiah

2 Kings chapters 18-20 records yet another interesting story about the power of staying connected. In the story, 2 Kings 18:13 we see that in the fourteenth year of King Hezekiah's reign, Sennacherib king of Assyria attacked all the fortified cities of Judah and captured them.

In the process, the king of Assyria the most powerful nation on earth at that time (equivalent to United States of America today) sent a letter to the king of Israel informing him of his intention to evade his city. In 2 Kings 19:14-19, the King of Israel Hezekiah, like King Jehoshaphat, went to God in prayer seeking His help against the enemy. I can only imagine the magnitude of the King's fear and worry. I can also envisage the fear that would engulf any King, President or Head of State of any country in Africa who has less military power to receive such a message from USA today. The good news to all believers is that if God is on your side, that is, if your eyes are on Him, the military power of your enemy does not count. It is meaningless because the Lord of Host is on your side; entrust any fight you are up against to Him and He will fight for you. Is your fight from your boss, workmate, mother or father in – law, sister or brother in – law? All you need is faith in God and focus on Him and you will not be disappointed. As He will ever be; He will fight for you.

Here is an account of 2 Kings19:14-19,"Hezekiah received the letter from the messengers and read it. Then he went up to the temple of the Lord and spread it out before the Lord. And Hezekiah prayed to the Lord: "O Lord, God of Israel, enthroned between the cherubim, you alone are God over all the kingdoms of the earth. You have made heaven and earth. Give ear, O Lord, and hear; open your eyes, O Lord, and see; listen to the words Sennacherib has sent to insult the living God. "It is true, O Lord, that the Assyrian kings have laid waste these nations and their lands. They have thrown their gods into the fire and destroyed them, for they were not gods but only wood and stone, fashioned by men's hands. Now, O Lord our God, deliver us from his hand, so that all kingdoms on earth may know that you alone, O Lord, are God."

As a result of the preceding verses God promised his people led by King Hezekiah, deliverance through the prophet Isaiah of which He (God) fulfilled his promise in 2 Kings 19:35-37. The Scripture says, "That night the angel of the Lord went out and put to death a hundred and eighty-five thousand men in the Assyrian camp. When the people got up the next morning—there were all the dead bodies! So Sennacherib king of Assyria broke camp and withdrew. He returned to Nineveh and stayed there. One day, while he was worshipping in the temple of his god Nisroch, his sons Adrammelech and Sharezer cut him down with the sword, and they escaped to the land of Ararat. And Esarhaddon his son succeeded him as king." When you stay connected to Him, I assure you that in any type of physical battle either sickness, marriage problems, or financial difficulties He will fight for you. However, you must pray and call on His name. Stay connected to Him by focusing on Him when faced with any challenges in life. He will equip you with the fortitude you need to defeat any enemy without you even throwing a punch.

Paul also expressed his confidence in God's protection as demonstrated when he wrote to the Church in Rome: "What, then, shall we say in response to this? If God is for us, who can be against us? He who did not spare his own Son, but gave him up for us all—how will he not also, along with him, graciously give us all things? Who will bring any charge against those whom God has chosen? It is God who justifies. Who is he that condemns? Christ Jesus, who died—more than that, who was raised to life—is at the right hand of God and is interceding for us," Romans 8:31-34. Praise God! It was an extraordinary act of love for Him to give away His only Son so sinful men could come to Him. Therefore, He is more than willing to take care and protect you (as a believer) from any enemy as endorsed by Paul. We read in 1 Samuel 17 that David (a young shepherd boy) killed Goliath (the Philistine giant) with a single stone. On the other hand, King Saul and all Israelites army including David's three big brothers, were gripped with fear, feeling powerless forgetting they had the Lord their God, the absolute champion on their side, David's eyes was on God who had assured his people of victory.

Provision

In spite of nine months of toil through pregnancy, some mothers can abandon their children for many reasons; perhaps they have found a new man or they did not plan to have children. Some give their children up for adoption because they could not care for them, or they want to lead a single life. Similarly, I have also known of fathers who do not care about what their children eat or wear, not contributing towards their maintenance even though they could afford it. These fathers fail to live up to their responsibility as men because of selfishness. I have also known of parents who have the desire to provide for their children but lack the means to do so, but God is a parent who is ever ready to provide for His children under any circumstances.

In Isaiah 49:15-16 the Bible says: "Can a woman forget her nursing child, And not have compassion on the son of her womb? Surely they may forget, Yet I will not forget you. See, I have inscribed you on the palms of My hands; Your walls are continually before Me." (NKJV)

Human beings have finite minds and therefore may do some things without proper preparation. One can a buy belt even though he has no trousers or shorts to put it through. Others also rush into things like marriage and businesses without proper preparation. Nevertheless, God can take care of us and provide everything we need; it does not matter where we are or what the situation be. God is not the irresponsible parent that I have described earlier, He is able and willing to provide for those whose eyes are on Him; those who look to Him for living, food, clothing and the other necessities of life. Scripture proves that God made arrangements and preparations for all the needs of mankind. He completed everything that was needed in advance of man's creation. So when man was created there was food to eat, water to drink and something to wear, all for his enjoyment. Therefore, it is imperative to focus on God since He cares for His children and will always provide for them.

He provided a ram for Abraham (Genesis 22:8-14); He provided food for the Israelites 40 years in the wilderness (Deuteronomy 29:5-6). This is why He is called Jehovah Jireh, the God who provides. Ignorance and lack of faith are some of the reasons why people think God does not care. They believe they can do it with their own ability without any help from God. This is the reason why it is stated in Psalm 127 that people rise up early in the morning and toil until late because of what they will eat and drink; they have excluded God - the life builder - so all that they strive for will be in vain. On other hand, the Psalmist states that God grants sleep to those he loves. This means He provides for those whose eyes are on Him and who have made Him the source of provision. When Jesus told His disciples how to pray He said, "When you pray to God your heavenly father, say give us this day our daily bread," Matthew 6:11 (NKJV).

David as a shepherd knew that the sheep totally depends on the shepherd for what they eat, drink, for where they sleep and protection. He gave a good description when he testified about God's pastoral role when he states, "The LORD is my shepherd; I shall not want. He makes me to lie down in green pastures; He leads me beside the still waters. He restores my soul; He leads me in the paths of righteousness For His name's sake. Yea, though I walk through the valley of the shadow of death, I will fear no evil; For You are with me; Your rod and Your staff, they comfort me. You prepare a table before me in the presence of my enemies; You anoint my head with oil; My cup runs over. Surely goodness and mercy shall follow me, All the days of my life; And I will dwell in the house of the LORD Forever". Psalms 23:1-6 (NKJV)

In the context of this subject God's provision to his children also extends to finances as well. God provides money for His children and wants them to prosper in money so trust Him to obtain all your material needs. Moses warned the children of Israel not to boast in anything (including wealth) they acquire when they get to the Promised Land for it is God who provides for all their need. He said: "You may say to yourself, "My power and the strength of my hands have produced this wealth for me". But remember the LORD your God, for it is he who gives you the ability to produce wealth, and so confirms his covenant, which he swore to your forefathers, as it is today," Deuteronomy 8:17-18.

Paul also wrote to the Corinthians when he was encouraging them to give generously. He said, "Now he who supplies seed to the sower and bread for food will also supply and increase your store of seed and will enlarge the harvest of your righteousness," 2 Corinthians 9:10.

Many people refuse to give to God's kingdom so they can effectively propagate the Gospel to help His work; they fear of running short of their substance such as money. In this scenario, Paul assured his readers that if they give to the Lord, He would give them back more than what they gave.

Christ focus or looking onto Christ eliminates fear

When Christ becomes the focus in your life there is no need to fear or be intimidated by any situation. The Bible states that God did not give us (believers) the spirit of fear and timidity but of boldness and sound mind (2 Timothy 1:7). The first century believers could stand against persecutions without fear because they focused on Christ. Here are some quotes, which illustrate the point.

Peter and John: 'Now when they saw the boldness of Peter and John, and perceived that they were uneducated and untrained men, they marveled. And they realized that they had been with Jesus. But Peter and John answered and said to them, "Whether it is right in the sight of God to listen to you more than to God, you judge. For we cannot but speak the things which we have seen and heard," Acts 4:13, 19-20 (NKJV).

Stephen: Brother Stephen faced death with joy and even prayed for God to forgive the sins of his killers because his eyes were on Jesus. Acts 7:55-60 (NKJV) says: "But he, being full of the Holy Spirit, gazed into heaven and saw the glory of God, and Jesus standing at the right hand of God. "Look! I see the heavens opened and the Son of Man standing at the right hand of God!" Then they cried out with a loud voice, stopped their ears, and ran at him with one accord; and they cast him out of the city and stoned him And the witnesses laid down their clothes at the feet of a young man named Saul. And they stoned Stephen as he was calling on God and saying, "Lord Jesus, receive my spirit." Then he knelt down and cried out with a loud voice, "Lord, do not charge them with this sin." And when he had said this, he fell asleep."

Stephen should be emulated when it comes to keeping focus on Christ; with your focus, you will see him and his glory. This will enable you to laugh in the midst of problems without blaming anyone and ask for forgiveness for those who may be the cause of your troubles. Many times unlike Stephen we take our eyes off Jesus the solution provider and begin to blame people that bring no solution but unbelief.

No room for pride for those whose eye is on Jesus Christ

Like fear, focusing on Jesus also eliminates pride, which is exhibited by a haughty attitude, arrogance, superiority and self-importance. It is an attitude displayed by those who believe often unjustifiably, that they are better than others because of what they have such as their money, qualifications or job position. But those whose eyes are on Jesus, that is those who have really seen Him and therefore receive Him as Lord and Saviour are always humble before God and men because they know that God is against pride as Solomon states; "Pride goes before destruction, And a haughty spirit before a fall. Better to be of a humble spirit with the lowly, than to divide the spoil with the proud." Proverbs 16:18-19 (NKJV)

There is a reason why the attitude of pride is not in those whose eyes are on Jesus, because he has become the centre of their life and has received the humility of his mind. Paul gave some stern advice when he states, "Your attitude should be the same as that of Christ Jesus, "Who, being in very nature God, did not consider equality with God something to be grasped but made himself nothing, taking the very nature of a servant, being made in human likeness. And being found in appearance as a man, he humbled himself and became obedient to death even death on a cross!" Philippians 2:5-8.

As he humbled himself and has been exalted, those whose eyes are on him and humble themselves will also be exalted as the Scripture says, "But He gives more grace. Therefore He says, "God resists the proud, but gives grace to the humble" James 4:6 (NKJV)

True humility demonstrated

Below are some people who demonstrated true humility when they met God or Jesus:

Isaiah: "In the year that King Uzziah died, I saw the Lord sitting on a throne, high and lifted up, and the train of His robe filled the temple. Above it stood seraphim; each one had six wings: with two he covered his face, with two he covered his feet, and with two he flew. And one cried to another and said: "Holy, holy, holy *is* the LORD of hosts; The whole earth *is* full of His glory!" And the posts of the door were shaken by the voice of him who cried out, and the house was filled with smoke. So I said: "Woe is me, for I am undone! Because I am a man of unclean lips, And I dwell in the midst of a people of unclean lips; For my eyes have seen the King, The LORD of hosts." Then one of the seraphim flew to me, having in his hand a live coal which he had taken with the tongs from the altar." Isaiah 6:1-6 (NKJV)

In my view, this story of the prophet shows that so many people claim to be Christians but have not known Christ. He is not the focus in their lives and this why they suffer with so much pride, panic and anxiety. The negative behaviour of many people in the church is a demonstration that they do not really know Christ; they have no connection with Him. When a person truly knows Him, there is a huge change in attitudes and behavior. It illustrates the bond they have established with Jesus the vine. Conversely, another point this highlights is that even though you are in church does not mean you are connected to Christ.

Peter humbles himself before Christ

Luke 5:1-12 is yet another example of humility by a person who has met with Christ. In Luke 5-6, Simon answered, "Master, we've worked hard all night and haven't caught anything. But because you say so, I will let down the nets." When they had done so, they caught such a large number of fish that their nets began to break." In verse 8, it states that when Simon Peter saw this, he fell at Jesus' knees and said, "Go away from me, Lord; I am a sinful man!" This does not mean he was chasing Jesus away from him as many others did. He was merely demonstrating his humility on realizing his unworthiness. In that situation, Peter did not think that he was worthy enough to talk to Jesus. If you are still arrogant though you are a Christian, humble yourself, the destructive power of pride is not the fruit of those who are connected to Christ. The story highlights that before Peter and his companions met Jesus they were doing things their own way, the traditional way, the way they know and caught nothing. Their experience yielded them no fruit but when they were connected to Him and did things as He instructed, things changed. There was a miracle; they caught so many fish that they had to ask assistance in order they could pull in their net.

Apostle John also fell at his feet in humility

Even though he was very close to him and loved by him, the one called "the disciple Jesus loved", when the glorious Jesus revealed himself to him in the island of Patmos John could not look at his face and fell at his feet in humility. Revelation 1: 17–18 says,"When I saw him, I fell at his feet as though dead. Then he placed his right hand on me and said, "Do not be afraid. I am the First and the Last. I am the Living One; I was dead, and behold I am alive for ever and ever! And I hold the keys of death and Hades."

Paul counted all things but loss when he saw him

When Christ is revealed to you, when he becomes your focus, if you rely on him you will count all things but loss. What I mean is that when this happens, everything except Christ will become of no value. Just like Paul, the things (materialism & vices) others are fighting for will mean nothing to you. These things will be insignificant to you knowing Christ and the power that raised him from the dead. Paul had something to say about himself after coming in contact with Christ. All Christians should emulate this as a good example of their genuine contact with Christ. It does not matter what you have achieved in life or the depth of your knowledge; the connection with Christ should be your top priority above everything else.

This is what Paul said in Philippians 3:4-10, "Though I myself have reasons for such confidence, if anyone else thinks he has reasons to put confidence in the flesh, I have more: circumcised on the eighth day, of the people of Israel, of the tribe of Benjamin, a Hebrew of Hebrews; in regard to the law, a Pharisee; as for zeal, persecuting the church; as for legalistic righteousness, faultless. But whatever was to my profit I now consider loss for the sake of Christ. What is more, I consider everything a loss compared to the surpassing greatness of knowing Christ Jesus my Lord, for whose sake I have lost all things. I consider them rubbish, that I may gain Christ and be found in him, not having a righteousness of my own that comes from the law, but that which is through faith in Christ—the righteousness that comes from God and is by faith. I want to know Christ and the power of his resurrection and the fellowship of sharing in his sufferings, becoming like him in his death."

Someone once asked me, "Pastor, does it mean when your eyes are on Christ or when he becomes your focus that you don't need money and other things? Nor that you don't have to work?" I replied, "Absolutely not! What it means is that all other things become secondary and Christ becomes the primary force in your life." My answer responded and corresponded with what Jesus said, "But seek first his kingdom and his righteousness, and all these things will be given to you as well."

Matthew 6:33. Many people have turned this quotation upside down and are seeking the things of this world first. The kingdom of God and the righteousness have become secondary or even irrelevant.

I remember trying to advise a friend years ago about being serious with God. He told me he wants to be rich first before he will be committed to God. His exact words were, "I want to be rich first so that if the Church needs money I can provide or even build a Church building for our Church". His intention - as it is for many people today- was good, but was turning the word of God upside down and was wrong. That was a good example of seeking first the things of this world. Sadly, the person I am talking about is dead; he never got rich nor was he able to build a church building for the church. The question is: What are you seeking first? What is your priority in life? Note that no one knows when death will come. Also, note that when death comes, no wealth you acquire will accompany you to the grave; it is your connection or relationship with Him, which will lead you to Him.

There is a reason why so many people are unstable in God. It is because they are looking to Christ and at the same time are being distracted by things of this world. Remember what Jesus said, "No-one can serve two masters. Either he will hate the one and love the other, or he will be devoted to the one and despise the other. You cannot serve both God and Money." Matthew 6:24 There is so much hatred, fighting and backbiting in the world today. Families and churches have not escaped the rage that drives this satanic force. This is happening because people are not looking to Christ as the source of all things but for positions and the things of this world of which the Bible says is here today and gone tomorrow.

1 John 2:15-17 says "Do not love the world or anything in the world. If anyone loves the world, the love of the Father is not in him. For everything in the world—the cravings of sinful man, the lust of his eyes and the boasting of what he has and does—comes not from the Father but from the

world. The world and its desires pass away, but the man who does the will of God lives forever."

Confession

When Christ is the focus of your life, this will change the nature of your confessions and what you pray for. Another effect of this will be that you will not engage in negative activity or thinking. Instead, you will direct your attention to praying positively about problems and other challenges in your life and the world. You will be positive in the things you say, give thanks and worship God for what He has done. All of this will be done with the knowledge that he is in control and will take care of everything. Similar to Paul, your heart desire is "that they may know Him and the power of His resurrection." What he meant was that we should not lose sight of Christ or take our eyes off him. Ensuring that we are connected to him and the power of his resurrection at all times. If Christ remains the focus, you will honour Him with your mouth and your heart; the place from which all your decisions and actions begin. It will enormously be difficult for others to disconnect you from his presence.

Those who focus on Christ and their eyes are on him will entrust the temperament of their ways to Him. They will honour Him with everything they have directed by Him as advised by Solomon, "Trust in the LORD with all your heart, and lean not on your own understanding. In all your ways acknowledge Him, and He shall direct your paths. Do not be wise in your own eyes; Fear the LORD and depart from evil. It will be health to your flesh, and strength to your bones. Honor the LORD with your possessions, And with the first fruits of all your increase. So your barns will be filled with plenty, and your vats will overflow with new wine." Proverbs 3:5-10 (NKJV)

"Whoever trusts in his riches will fall, but the righteous will thrive like a green leaf," Proverbs 11:28.

"Commit your works to the LORD, And your thoughts will be established." Proverbs 16:3 (NKJV)

The above quotations emphasize that when God or Christ is the centre of a person's heart, the focus of that individual's affairs are controlled by the Lord. The person will experience success and prosperity in everything he or she does.

Examples of true focus and the results

It is easy to consider the intensity of your situation and immediately conclude it is all over - in other words – you have given up. This is not the right option for a believer. In my view, believers are missing one of the fundamental advantages at our disposal - the Word of God. A lot of us are failing to consult it before reaching a conclusion on any matter. The Bible is God's word; and we as Christians believe that it has the answer to every situation or question in human life. Therefore, we must always consult the word of God to see what it says about our situation before we finally decide what to do. The Bible informs us about who God is, his ways and all that He can do. It gives us guidance on how we live our lives, encouragement and warns us about what is dangerous and evil. Paul wrote to Timothy stating, "All Scripture is God-breathed and is useful for teaching, rebuking, correcting and training in righteousness," 2 Timothy 3:16.

2 Peter 1:3-4 states, "His divine power has given us everything we need for life and godliness through our knowledge of him who called us by his own glory and goodness. Through these he

has given us his very great and precious promises, so that through them you may participate in the divine nature and escape the corruption in the world caused by evil desires."

Here Peter also had message for his readers and believers; he said what stands between believers and everything they require in life is the knowledge that God's power has already provided us with everything we need, this includes the exact things we need to live a godly life. God's word underpins this power, so it is crucial to read and engage it fervently. Another advantage of the word of God is the fact that it helps us to take lessons from how God related to the people of the olden time in both positive and in negative ways.

Paul uses Israel's history as a warning to the Corinthian church as he said in 1 Corinthians 10:11-12 "These things happened to them as examples and were written down as warnings for us, on whom the fulfillment of the ages has come. So, if you think you are standing firm, be careful that you don't fall." When you know the Lord is with you, that connection gives you the courage and joy to go through every challenge in life. Of which every man and woman is bound to face here on earth.

Joseph's story: Genesis 39:1-6

Joseph is one example of someone whose eyes was on God and as a result reaped the result because he prospered and succeeded in everything he did in a foreign land. He did it despite facing one of the greatest temptations any man can ever face in life. He received the benefit or the power of focusing on God, which in the context of this book is the power of staying connected to God or Christ. "Now Joseph had been taken down to Egypt. Potiphar, an Egyptian who was one of Pharaoh's officials, the captain of the guard, bought him from the Ishmaelites who had taken him there. The LORD was with Joseph and he ***prospered,*** and he lived in the house of his Egyptian master. When his master saw that the LORD was with him and that the LORD gave him ***success*** in everything he did, Joseph found favour in his eyes and became his attendant. Potiphar put him in charge of his household, and he entrusted to his care everything he owned. From the time he put him in charge of his household and of all that he owned, the LORD blessed the household of the

Egyptian because of Joseph. The blessing of the LORD was on everything Potiphar had, both in the house and in the field. So he left in Joseph's care everything he had; with Joseph in charge, he did not concern himself with anything except the food he ate. Now Joseph was well-built and handsome,"

The background of the story highlights that:

1. Joseph was sold twice. After he has been sold by his brothers he was again sold to Potiphar by the Ishmaelites

    I reckon that his connection with God made him into an excellent businessman; he was like some key spare parts we use to call 'the blood tonic' when I was a spare parts dealer in Ghana years ago. In those days when you had those kinds of parts, you would offer a lot of money for them because they were vital parts. Joseph's story is even good for preachers. I have used his story to preach under the following themes:

    ✦ God's faithfulness–Joseph remained faithful to God because whatever the Lord says, He fulfils it; as his dream came true

- How to be successful in overcoming temptation using his method, he ran from sin
- The results of being grateful; he was grateful to the Lord ,so refused to sin against him
- Recently I listened to a preacher who also used his story to preach on "Never share your dream with anybody for not all people are happy to see you prosper" I think this is a good advice that will save many from a problem similar to the one faced by Joseph.

2. Joseph's Sojourn: When he ended up in a foreign land, his father was told a wild animal had killed him. I can only imagine the shock of his aging father when he heard the news of his death. Sold to a foreign land, he lost his family, friends, country, language and perhaps his favorite food.

There is a very important point here and the key to my message; that is despite his situation the Bible says that although he had lost everything else he still had God. As a result of God being with him, he prospered and succeeded in everything he did as we noticed in Verse 23 of the opening scripture, against all odds. Another equally important point is that though Joseph was a slave in a foreign land. The Bible says he prospered both in the house and in the field. This is due to the fact the he remained connected to God. We read that his master noted Joseph's success he had been affected since Joseph arrived in his house because the Bible says," the blessing of the LORD was on everything he had, both in the house and in the field so he left everything he had for him." Perhaps to make him more prosperous who knows?

Now let us relate this story to our own lives. Now consider your own situation and compare it with that of Joseph's and answer these few questions:

- ✦ What have you lost in life?
- ✦ Who is or how many have conspired against you?
- ✦ Who has deserted or disappointed you? The worse part of this is that it could be someone whom you have helped or cared for or someone who is supposed to protect you.

I believe that unlike Joseph, 99.9% of people who have traveled to UK or any other country to settle, have done so by choice or willingly. 99 percent of us were not sold, captured or forced to do so against our will. In fact, some of us had to fast for days may be weeks or months, others sold their businesses and properties and found other means to travel. However, do not forget that Joseph got to Egypt after been sold by his own jealous brothers. As I often emphasize, it is not easy to deal with the loss of your pet; I remember the mood of a man and his family when the pet dog they had for sixteen years died. I know personally how difficult and painful it is when you have to part company with someone you have been with for a long time. It could be a friend, husband or wife, a girl or boyfriend. I remember how I wept one night like a baby in the presence of a girl in my early Christian life. I had to end the relationship with her because I had seen the light of God and wanted to live a Godly life. It was not easy but thank God I was able to do it through His divine power as Peter said in 2 Peter 1:3 "His divine power has given us everything we need for life and godliness through our knowledge of him who called us by his own glory and goodness".

I am sure that the day Joseph was sold by his brothers was the worse day in his life. I imagine him turning to his brothers for the last time, bound in chains before he was taken away. I also believe that while he was sad, helpless and without defense, his evil brothers were happy knowing that they have got rid of him and his dream as it is recorded in Genesis 37:19-20: "Here comes that dreamer!" they said to each other. "Come now, let's kill him and throw him into one of these cisterns and say that a ferocious animal devoured him. Then we'll see what comes of his dreams."

This point of Joseph's ordeal always reminds me of a song we used to sing years ago. It could have been a fitting song sang by Joseph's brothers at that time. In fact, I always sing this song any time I preach on this subject.

It goes like this:

You are the one among us that our father loved than anyone of us

You are the one among us that our father loved than anyone of us
Once we have got you, once we have laid hands on you
We will sell you to merchants
Once we have got you, once we have laid hands on you
We will sell you to merchants

Returning to the Joseph story; what his brothers did not know was that even though they had sold him or parted company with him, he was still connected to God. While they sang: "We have sold you because our father loves you more than all of us" I believe because of his faith and connection with God Joseph was also singing another equally fitting song which related to his situation (which I also sing during preaching):

Which goes like this:

He is precious to me than anything in the world
Even if the whole world deserts me
Having God/Jesus is everything
He is precious to me than anything in the world

I want you to take a few minutes to reflect on the meaning of both songs and see which one relates to your situation. Is anyone rejoicing and singing the same song sang by Joseph's brothers because they thought they have 'got' or finished you? What is your song at this time as you respond? Are you overwhelmed by their deed or are you rejoicing and singing the same song as the one I presumed Joseph sang? It could have been the key to his victory and it could be the key to your victory too.

Another equally important point is that there is no doubt that God was with him, in other words his heart was right with God. Brethren, no No matter what your ambition or the size of your dream, the state of your heart, your relationship with God, and your connection with Him is very important. I believe God was with Joseph because of the state of his heart and relationship with Him. He led a clean life and did not give himself up to alcohol, bad habits or bad company because he had lost everything. He did not do what probably most people would do today when faced with serious problems in life. He stayed loyal to God, kept his composure and kept his eyes on Him. If anyone doubts Joseph's loyalty to God I would say he proved that his heart was right with God when he refused to sin or go to bed with his master's wife as stated in Genesis 39:10-12, "And though she spoke to Joseph day after day, he refused to go to bed with her or even to be with her. One day he went into the house to attend to his duties, and none of the household servants was inside. She caught him by his cloak and said, "Come to bed with me!" But he left his cloak in her hand and ran out of the house".

Many of us do not prosper or succeed in life because the Lord is not with us. This is even though we may call ourselves Christians, our hearts are not right with him – we sin and do so many things against God. Some of our actions bring shame to Him; it gives chance to the enemies of God to blasphemy against the name of God (2 Samuel 12:14; Isaiah 52:5; Romans 2:23-24). Brethren, it is important to note that God was not with Joseph just because he was a Jew or Israelite. Similarly, He will be with you not because you call yourself a Christian. If you show your total commitment to God through faith in Christ He will stick by you in the most difficult and challenging times.

Even though Joseph had a dream from God, he would have been ignored if he had allowed himself to be overtaken by the problem and given himself up to the world. This is in the context of losing everything and therefore contaminating himself with the things of the world. God promised to be with so many people including Kings in the Old Testament but when some of them failed to honour their part of the agreement He left them. It is vital to stay loyal to God even if you lose everything and everyone, he will always be there as He promised.

Many people may have started well with God but like Samson, they have lost the Spirit of God; they have lost connection with Him and so they are now struggling in life. Judges 16:20-21 says, "Then she called, "Samson, the Philistines are upon you!" *He awoke from his sleep and thought, "I'll go out* as before and shake myself free". **He did not know that the Lord had left him** so consequently he was arrested because he was depleted of the strength **to defend himself. "Then the Philistines seized** him, gouged out his eyes and took him down to Gaza. Binding him with bronze shackles, they set him to grinding in the prison".

There is good news coupled with my message of consolation; when you truly know and understand what it means to remain in Him. You will remain connected to Him, irrespective of what people say or do against you; He is your shield and protector, far greater and stronger than any number of people put together. Paul said, "What, then, shall we say in response to this? If God is for us, who can be against us?" Romans 8:31. In reply, what do you think Paul was talking about here? Before then in verse 35 he said "Shall trouble or hardship or persecution or famine or nakedness or danger or sword?" In Roman 8:37-39, "No, in all these things we are more than conquerors through him who loved us. For I am convinced that neither death nor life, neither angels nor demons, neither the present nor the future, nor any powers. Neither height nor depth, nor anything else in all creation, will be able to separate us from the love of God that is in Christ Jesus our Lord".

Elisha knew that God was with him so he did not panic but prayed the Lord would strike the Aramean Army with blindness in 2 Kings 6:15-18, "When the servant of the man of God got up and went out early the next morning, an army with horses and chariots had surrounded the city. "Oh, my lord, what shall we do?" the servant asked. "Don't be afraid," the prophet answered. "Those who are with us are more than those who are with them." And Elisha prayed, "O Lord, open his eyes so that he may see." Then the Lord opened the servant's eyes, and he looked and saw the hills full of horses and chariots of fire all round Elisha. As the enemy came down towards him, Elisha prayed to the Lord, "Strike these people with blindness".

Why am I saying all these things? It is vital that you know about the power of staying connected so that you can stay attached to Him irrespective of what it takes. I am comfortable in what I am saying, because in my personal experience - as a Ghanaian proverb says – 'I have carried water, have also carried palm wine and now I know which one of them is the heavier of the two'. I know what the Lord has done for me and I know what he is capable of doing. Like David, we must also in our testing experiences call all people to come and taste the goodness of the Lord. He said: "Oh, taste and see that the Lord is good; Blessed is the man who trusts in Him." Psalms 34:8 (NKJV)

Many people adopt bad attitudes and habits because of the negative situations in their lives or what people have done to them. Some turn to alcohol and engage in immoral activities as result of the painful emotions associated with such experiences. Other people respond this way with believing it is retaliation against those who offended them. In fact, they are inflicting more harm or damage on their mental and physical state. In most cases, men and women who divorce begin to lead immoral lives; the main intention is about proving to their former partners that they are still desirable. This of course, is not only irresponsible but also selfish and the most ridiculous way to prove yourself to others.

The most disturbing part of this state of affairs is when some people blame God for their problems and some even stop attending church. As you read this book I want you to take a lesson from Joseph who did not allow the situation to drive him from God. Instead, he stayed loyal and connected until God was glorified in his life. Do not give yourself to the enemy, do not mess yourself up, do not go out of your way to prove to a person your existence or that you are desirable by engaging in self-degrading behavior. God has made you somebody when you were born, and he will continue to fulfill his promises if you stay connected to Him. So do not rush into a relationship, which may not be the will of God. This way God can provide, lead and protect you as a shepherd cares for his sheep.

Some people are uncomfortable when in places where they are not known, is unfamiliar to them or if they are not with other church members. Others suffer the said consequence when they are away from their family members, wives or husbands. These people are Christians only when they are in a place where they are known. They fail to declare their Christianity or their faith in a places where they are unknown.

Joseph's example has shown that even though he was away from his own people of the same faith, he abided or remained in God who honoured him. Through Joseph's experience, you can see what is important in your own life. It is not what you have lost or who have parted or is parting company with you, but what and who is left with you. The three Hebrew captives, Shadrach, Meshach and Abednego would not defile themselves with the food and things of Babylon; they would not worship King Nebuchadnezzar's golden image and as a result were thrown into a furnace of fire.

However, God was with them in the fire, the king saw it himself and testified about it. This caused him (the king) to declare that the whole province must only worship the God of Shadrach, Meshach and Abednego. Daniel 3:24-26 states: "Then King Nebuchadnezzar leaped to his feet in amazement and asked his advisers "Weren't there three men that we tied up and threw into the fire?" They replied, "Certainly, O king." He said, "Look! I see four men walking around in the fire, unbound and unharmed, and the fourth looks like a son of the gods." Nebuchadnezzar then approached the opening of the blazing furnace and shouted, "Shadrach, Meshach and Abednego, servants of the Most High God, come out! Come here!" So Shadrach, Meshach and Abednego came out of the fire"

Daniel 3:28-30 concludes the interesting story. It said "Then Nebuchadnezzar said, "Praise be to the God of Shadrach, Meshach and Abednego, who has sent his angel and rescued his servants! They trusted in him and defied the king's command and were willing to give up their lives rather than serve or worship any god except their own God. Therefore I decree that the people of any nation or language who say anything against the God of Shadrach, Meshach and Abednego be cut into pieces and their houses be turned into piles of rubble, for no other god can save in this way." Then the king promoted Shadrach, Meshach and Abednego in the province of Babylon".

"Daniel also in the days of King Darius refused to pray in the name of the King was and thrown into the lion's den. The Lord delivered and honoured him for his commitment to Him. The scripture says, "Now when Daniel learned that the decree had been published, he went home to his upstairs room where the windows opened towards Jerusalem. Three times a day he got down on his knees and prayed, giving thanks to his God, just as he had done before. Then these men went as a group and found Daniel praying and asking God for help," Daniel 6:10-11. So the king gave the order, and they brought Daniel and threw him into the lions' den.

The king said to Daniel, "May your God, whom you serve continually, rescue you!" A stone was brought and placed over the mouth of the den, and the king sealed it with his own signet ring and with the rings of his nobles, so that Daniel's situation might not be changed, Daniel 6:16-17.

"At the first light of dawn, the king got up and hurried to the lions' den. When he came near the den, he called to Daniel in an anguished voice, "Daniel, servant of the living God, has your God, whom you serve continually, been able to rescue you from the lions?" Daniel answered, "O king, live forever! My God sent his angel, and he shut the mouths of the lions. They have not hurt me, because I was found innocent in his sight. Nor have I ever done any wrong before you, O king." Daniel 6:19-22

Remember that all these men were ordinary men, even captives living in foreign land. They are similar to many people today living in foreign lands, a place where no one could have noticed their presence or activities. In spite of this, they knew they served an Omnipresent and Omniscient God. At this point, I would like to ask you some variable questions: where are you now? What are you doing? Just like the men mentioned above, does your actions promote or defend Christ and confirm that you are a Christian? Does it mark you out as a person who has connection with Christ as the name of a Christian denotes? Unlike Joseph, the three men and Daniel, many people would have given in to the demands of the people at that time to save their lives. Others would have pleased men (universal) which would have been a wrong option damaging their relationship with God. I would advise that whatever difficulty, threat or reproach you may face, stay connected to God. You should never abandon God or your faith for the fear or favour of men and He would also reciprocate; it is a promise to those who trust in Him as stated in His Word (Deuteronomy 31:6; Joshua 1:5; Hebrews 13:5)

Years ago, in another town far away from my own, in the dead of night, I was awoken and asked to come outside. Surprisingly, I came out to see three women, one of whom informed me that one of them could be my comfort for the night. In other words, I should go and sleep with one of them. Without any doubt, many men would have seen this offer as one of the biggest opportunities in their life. However, thank God, with the help of the Holy Spirit I immediately saw it as a temptation and sin against God. I thanked her very much for such concern in my personal affairs, and the offer of this beautiful lady, but I could not accept it. I then quickly reminded her that the Bible states: "Everything is permissible but not everything is beneficial," 1 Corinthians 10:23. These women looked at one another in utter disbelief and shame; I politely asked permission to leave their presence and went back to bed. What would you have done as a man in this type of temptation? I have met similar types of temptations in my life before and after I got married. Nevertheless, thank God, I have come out victorious each time because of my connection with Jesus Christ, He is also willing and able to help you in the same way. This is why the Lord has given me a woman who has all the qualities a man can ask for praise His name.

I wrote this book in London in UK where I now live. I have heard the stories of many people who were on fire for God when they were in their native countries but sadly when these same people migrated to the United Kingdom these individuals have abandoned their God. They are now doing all sorts of things detested by God. The worse part of it is when those who left their wives and husbands behind in the name of hardship have neglected and abandon those they left behind for unacceptable reasons and are defiling themselves. They have forgotten those who have helped and cared for them previously because of the awful lives they now live. In extreme cases, I have also heard some of these people even teasing the faithful believers about their integrity and loyalty to God. If any of the above describes your case please make a U-turn to God before it is too late, for no one knows when Jesus will be coming back.

David also knowing that God was with him said:

"The LORD is my shepherd; I shall not be in want. He makes me lie down in green pastures, he leads me beside quiet waters, he restores my soul. He guides me in paths of righteousness for his name's sake. Even though I walk through the valley of the shadow of death, I will fear no evil, for you are with me; your rod and your staff, they comfort me. You prepare a table before me in the presence of my enemies. You anoint my head with oil; my cup overflows. Surely goodness and love will follow me all the days of my life, and I will dwell in the house of the LORD forever." Psalms 23:1-6

David as a shepherd knew how the sheep depend on its shepherd for everything. He considered himself a sheep and the Lord as his shepherd. In verse 1 and 2 he said because he's in the care of the Lord - his shepherd - he will provide for him anything he wanted, that is, what to eat and wear, even when he has lost his job. When you know that God is with you, like David, you have the confidence in Him to provide everything you need, just as sheep have confidence in the shepherd.

On their way to make, a sacrifice Abraham told Isaac God would provide the ram for the sacrifice. The scripture says, Isaac spoke up and said to his father Abraham, "Father?" "Yes, my son?" Abraham replied, "The fire and wood are here," Isaac, said "but where is the lamb for the burnt offering?" Abraham answered, "God himself will provide the lamb for the burnt offering, my son. And the two of them went on together," Genesis 22:7-8.Indeed, God provided the ram for the sacrifice: Genesis 22:11-13 says: "But the angel of the LORD called out to him from heaven, "Abraham! Abraham!" "Here I am," he replied. "Do not lay a hand on the boy," he said. "Do not do anything to him. Now I know that you fear God, because you have not withheld from me your son, your only son." Abraham looked up and there in a thicket he saw a ram caught by its horns. He went over and took the ram and sacrificed it as a burnt offering instead of his son."

In Psalm 23:3, David talked about a time when one needs direction in life I mean decision time. David said, "In these periods the Lord brings me back to Him and guides me how to live and do what is right so that I may bring glory to his name." Whenever you submit to His will, he will also give you direction. James said, "If any of you lacks wisdom, he should ask God, who gives generously to all without finding fault, and it will be given to him." James 1:5

Psalm 23:4 is about the Lord's protection and deliverance, his security. David said 'he protects or delivers me from the shadows of death' because he was covered by the shepherd. When a shepherd goes out with the sheep and they are tired and asleep, he stays awake to watch over them. David said in the midst of danger he feared nothing because his Lord, the shepherd was with him. Therefore, I say to all those who have their eyes on Jesus not to fear the following dangers or challenges when you:

- ✦ Have a serious or life-threatening illness, in an operating theatre
- ✦ Have been involved in an accident
- ✦ Have been attacked by robbers or by someone in a fight
- ✦ You are a woman about to give birth to a child or a woman in labor
- ✦ Witches and wizard takes your soul to meetings intending to kill your physical form while you are sleeping
- ✦ Someone takes your soul or body to a juju man with the intention to kill or destroy you

In Psalm23:5, David says 'you will glorify me before my enemies'. This means that for all believers, your enemies will be present to witness your day of victory and success. The reason for this is that the good shepherd, the captain of host has never lost a battle. Mordecai was honoured while his enemy Haman was killed in his place as stated in the book of Esther."So Haman got the robe and the horse. He robed Mordecai, and led him on horseback through the city streets, proclaiming before him: "This is what is done for the man the king delights to honour!" Esther 6:11 for the full story read from Verse 1.

Finally, in Psalm 23:6 David said when you are with God, he accompanies wherever you go with his goodness, love and mercies. "Because of all these benefits, I in return promise to be in your house forever," said David. Let us return to the theme of this book by asking these questions, is God with you? Are you connected to him? in the context of the Joseph's story and my message, like him:

- ✦ You may have lost your job
- ✦ You may have lost your husband, wife or your child through death, divorce or rebellion. Even in some cases you may have lost these people because your situation changed e.g. when you lost your job
- ✦ You may have lost your boy/girl friend or some friends.
- ✦ You may have stopped associating with a dreadful character because you wanted to live a godly life and this has caused you to go through a very difficult time.

- ✦ You may have failed your school examination as a student or your driving test this time round
- ✦ You may have been refused a visa or application for a residency permit in the foreign land (where you now live)
- ✦ May be it is someone you trusted and thought that this person would not have been the one to desert and disappoint you. Many times this happens to ministers and leaders of churches as often those we trust forsake us.
- ✦ You may be like David walking through the valley of the shadow of death, facing a dreadful challenge.

What more could be said about this as these are the problems of everyday life. People will always disappoint, betray, or hate others for their bad habits. The good news is that none of this matters; what matters is that your heart will allow God to dwell in you. Joseph lost everything and everybody except God, the unseen, the omnipresent and omniscient God. Again, I say, "what matters is not what you have lost but what you have." God was with Joseph and he rose up to become Prime Minister in a foreign land even though he had lost everything. Through my experience and the word of God, in most cases, losing these things and these people could open doors to your destiny as reinforced by Paul: "And we know that in all things God works for the good of those who love him, who have been called according to his purpose." Romans 8:28

The Devil will always use people who try to bring about your death, disaster, or even your downfall. However if God is with you He will turn every situation for your good. Later in Joseph's story, he told his brothers when they bowed before him, "You intended to harm me, but God intended it for good to accomplish what is now being done, the saving of many lives." Genesis 50:20

Can I ask you some very important questions: If you had to lose all physical, material things and everybody on earth; if you were to find yourself in the valley of shadow of death left with nothing, like Joseph. Who lost everything and everybody and later found himself in a foreign land, what will you be left with? Will you be left with God or you have already lost Him too like Samson as I said earlier on. This physically powerful man was in grave danger and needed God most when he fell in the hands of his enemies but could not find his strength because the Spirit had left him as we read in Judges 16:20-21. Then she called: "Samson, the Philistines are upon you!" He awoke from his sleep and thought, "I'll go out as before and shake myself free." But he did not know that the Lord had left him. Then the Philistines seized him, gouged out his eyes and took him down to Gaza. Binding him with bronze shackles, they set him to grinding in the prison". This is the most dangerous thing that could happen to any man or woman on this earth - to lose everything including God. Let Joseph be an encouragement to anyone who may be in a situation where you seemed to have lost everything except God, do not leave Him, hold on to Him. Stay connected to Him and he will prove Himself to you as did for Joseph.

Is Christ In Your Crisis?

Seeing God in any crisis that you face in life is the first step to winning any battle you may face. It is unfortunate that many Christians when faced with crisis even forget that they serve the Almighty God who is able to do everything and they act like people who have no hope. When you see God in your crisis, you turn to Him for your way out. Crisis is a dangerous or a worrying time: a situation or period in which things are very uncertain, difficult, or painful, especially a time when action must be taken to avoid complete disaster or breakdown. It is also a critical moment: a time when something very important for the future happens or is decided, a time of great danger, difficulty and anxiety in life e.g. financial, in health, family issues etc.

In other words, a crisis can be seen as going through a very difficult time. There is also the implication that it is solvable if one finds the right way or help to resolve it. In the context of this book, the right way is when is you stay connected to God. Therefore, our crisis, in the context of our theme, is our time of great danger, difficulty and anxiety in life, which could be any of the few below:

- ✦ In my view, the number one crisis in anybody's life is when a person is without Christ; a time when a person is not born again, a time when a person is spiritually disconnected from God.
- ✦ A time when we face financial difficulty
- ✦ The difficult period of bringing up our children
- ✦ The difficult time when our marriage is in crisis, which can cause severe damage or serious breakdown in the relationship, or also the time when one searching for a partner
- ✦ A time when it is difficult to make decisions
- ✦ When one is facing immigration problems in a foreign country
- ✦ When people hate you even though you have done nothing wrong them
- ✦ A time of job loss or lack of a job

Everyone on the face of this earth faces crisis or challenges like some of those mentioned above. Life is not free of crisis or challenges; we are all vulnerable, but as I said before - every crisis is solvable when the victim of that crisis is connected to Christ.

Why do I have to have Christ in my crisis?

If that is your question, God is the only one who does not need anyone's help or depend on anybody because He is self-sufficient. As a man (universal) you need Christ in every area of your life. Firstly, we need His salvation as no one can save himself. Secondly, we need Him in times of crisis or challenges (in need of provision, direction and security as David said in Psalm 23). These crisis or challenges are bound to come to every man at some point in life whether a believer or not. Therefore, we all need the help of Christ in these times. This is why Jesus encourages believers to stay connected to him when He said that without Him, no one could do anything. Remember the foundation Scripture of this book. "I am the vine; you are the branches. If a man remains in me and I in him, he will bear much fruit; apart from me you can do nothing" John 15:5. This means that as a believer you cannot solve these crisis and challenges without Jesus' help. A problem becomes solvable when one stays connected to Christ the vine.

King Solomon paints the same picture when he said, Trust in the Lord with all your heart and lean not on your own understanding; in all your ways acknowledge him, and he will make your paths straight. Proverbs 3:5-6

Having God in your crisis is to acknowledge Him in these times. Solomon said when you acknowledge him he will make your paths straight or He will direct your ways (as some translation will put it). He will show you the way out. Acknowledging him in your crisis is also saying to him; "Lord I cannot do it on my own please help me to do it." The good news is that God is more than willing to help all those who call on him in times of crisis. The Scripture said in the books of Jeremiah and Hebrews respectively, "Call to me and I will answer you and tell you great and unsearchable things you do not know." Jeremiah 33:3.

"Therefore, since we have a great high priest who has gone through the heavens, Jesus the Son of God, let us hold firmly to the faith we profess. For we do not have a high priest who is unable to sympathize with our weaknesses, but we have one who has been tempted in every way, just as we are yet was without sin. Let us then approach the throne of grace with confidence, so that we may receive mercy and find grace to help us in our time of need." Hebrews 4:14-16

Peter also advices young men,"Humble yourselves, therefore, under God's mighty hand, that he may lift you up in due time. Cast all your anxiety on him because he cares for you." 1 Peter 5:6-7

Remember also that Christ has promised never to leave us or forsake us"…And surely I am with you always, to the very end of the age." Matthew 28:20

Keep your lives free from the love of money and be content with what you have, because God has said, "Never will I leave you; never will I forsake you. Hebrews 13:5

Examples of God's or Christ's presence in crisis

Abram's crisis with Lot: 'So Abram said to Lot, "Let's not have any quarrelling between you and me, or between your herdsmen and mine, for we are brothers. Is not the whole land before you? Let's part company. If you go to the left, I'll go to the right; if you go to the right, I'll go to the left." Lot looked up and saw that the whole plain of the Jordan was well watered, like the garden of the LORD, like the land of Egypt, towards Zoar. (This was before the LORD destroyed Sodom and Gomorrah.) So Lot chose for himself the whole plain of the Jordan and set out towards the east. The two men parted company: Abram lived in the land of Canaan, while Lot lived among the cities of the plain and pitched his tents near Sodom.' Genesis 13:8-12

The story above shows that men (universal) may part company with you, or deny you. They may choose what seems like a better location in their eyes and leave you all alone with what they think is the least better. They may see what they left behind as a poor location, but if God is with you, He is more than able to transform anything. He can turn the least of what you have got into greatness. Lot had the well-watered land, but Abraham had God's promise which led him to many blessings. You may have been cheated or deceived by or someone after committing your time, money, wisdom or resources into a project or business and when the time to enjoy the fruits of your work arrived, you were kicked out. You may have labored with a man or woman to build a future, but when you were supposed to reap the dividends of your labour, you were shown the exit. Worst of all, someone comes along and enjoys the fruits of your labour. This situation happens to many women who suffered with their men at the beginning of their relationship. When some of these unfaithful and wicked men get into high positions through the help of these women, they say they want a woman to match their standard. The truth being the woman who sacrificed her time and resources in an effort to support him to achieve his ambitions and success was not able to improve herself at the same time. So the woman is no longer up to his standard. The women then suffer the humiliation of divorce and the man leaves to marry a new woman.

One of the above scenarios may apply to your situation and like Abram when he faced the crisis of Lot choosing the better part of the land so you feel distressed. You may have helped someone who has later disappointed you. You may have been treated similar to Abram's experience with Lot who having got all that he had through Abram, paid him back with ungratefulness. The truth is that Lot only got to the disputed land because God told Abram to go there and he went with him. Out of courtesy and peace, Abram gave Lot first choice to pick the piece of a land he wanted, in order to settle the dispute. Out of Abram's sight, Lot chose the most fertile part of the land because he was greedy and disrespectful. I would say that Lot definitely took advantage of Abram's humility and wholehearted character. If many people in the world today will possess the same heart as Abram, many unnecessary disputes in our societies, families, and even in our churches would be eliminated.

The good news is that although Lot thought he had the better and the fertile part of the land and Abram was supposed to get the worse part of the land what he did not know was that Abram had God's promise (God's blessings) with him. Abram was connected to God through the promise as stated in Scripture: "The Lord had said to Abram,

"Leave your country, your people and your father's household and go to the land I will show you." I will make you into a great nation and I will bless you; I will make your name great, and you will be a blessing. I will bless those who bless you, and whoever curses you I will curse; and all peoples on earth will be blessed through you." Genesis 12:1-3

Below is the brief synopsis of what happened to each of them after they were separated:

Abram

- ✦ The Lord came and spoke to him, to lift up his eyes to see the land He (God) will give to him and his descendants
- ✦ He changed his name from Abram to Abraham meaning the father of many
- ✦ He received his promised son Isaac
- ✦ The Lord swore by His name to bless him after he was obediently ready to sacrifice Isaac at God's request.

Lot

- Was captured in battle
- Had to flee with his family from Sodom
- His wife turned to a pillar of salt because she refused to heed to God's instructions, 'don't look back'
- He slept with both his daughters under the influence of alcohol and had children with them.

What am I saying here? I want to encourage you that even if everything is taken away from you, make sure you do not lose Christ also. As one songwriter said that with God or Christ, you have everything. There is a saying among Ghanaians, which says, "If you and someone own something together and it includes God. When it's time to share it, if that person keeps the part which includes God, giving you the other part, then that person has cheated. The person is giving you something without God so you must ask that person to share it again." The truth of the matter is you do not need anything or anybody to prosper and succeed. However, you need God first; everything else is secondary. Jesus in his Sermon on the Mount said, "But seek first his kingdom and his righteousness, and all these things will be given to you as well," Matthew 6:33.

With the above story I ask you to lift up your eyes just as the Lord told Abram.

What do you see?

Do you see God with you or not?

Abram lost the best of the land (his crisis) but because he had God when he lifted his eyes he saw the Promised Land. I pray that instead of seeing your crisis you will also see your Promised Land as you lift your eyes.

Disciples' in a boat crisis: "Then he got into the boat and his disciples followed him. Without warning, a furious storm came up on the lake, so that the waves swept over the boat. But Jesus was sleeping. The disciples went and woke him, saying, "Lord, save us! We're going to drown!" He replied, "You of little faith, why are you so afraid?" Then he got up and rebuked the winds and the waves, and it was completely calm. The men were amazed and asked, "What kind of man is this? Even the winds and the waves obey him!" Matthew 8:23-27

In the above story, we see that the disciples faced a crisis; they faced a storm even though Christ was with them. This means and confirms what I said earlier, that even though you are a Christian and you fasted or prayed, crisis will still come. Being a Christian does not make you crisis-free as many believe, but thank God, because the disciples turned to or invited Christ (who was with them in the boat) he spoke to calm the situation thus resolving the crisis. Christ will also do the same for you if you will turn to him in your crisis because he has power over any crisis or situation. Like the disciples, we also often encounter storms, crisis or challenges in life. Sometimes we feel like it is all over because we have been pushed to the wall. The truth is when we truly understand who Christ is, and what He is able to do, we will realize that not only does He control the storms of nature but also every storm of life you may face. The power of Jesus that calmed the storm for the disciples is also available and can also help you to deal with any problems or crisis in your life. Jesus is willing to help if you only ask him or acknowledge him in your crisis. Be encouraged with this fact that he knows every detail of your life.

This first story of the disciples also shows that Christ must not only be our saviour but also our Lord. This means that when you receive Christ as Saviour, you must also ask Him or acknowledge Him to take control or be master of your life. Just as Christ was with the disciples in the boat he'll be with you. Remember that Christ reacted to the storm only after the apostles have asked for His help. In the same way He will not act until you have invited him - that means you have acknowledged him.

A story of a christian woman

There was a Christian woman who once received the best visitor every believer would like to have - the person was Jesus Christ. After offering him a seat, there was a knock at the door; the woman went out to answer the door. She was met with blows from Satan who had been knocking; she rushed to the living room where Jesus was sitting. The second time the woman went to open the door and was met with stronger blows. In tears and in pain she rushed back to the living room again, this time she asked Jesus why He sat down and watched her being beaten by Satan. She thought He should have tackled Satan because He was stronger than him. Jesus told her, "When I came to your house, you gave me a seat but you did not ask me to take control of the house that is why I did not answer the door". Immediately the woman said, "everything is in your hand, take charge."

When the knock came, the third time, this time Jesus Christ was in charge of the house; He opened the door to Satan who probably thought it was the woman again. When he saw Jesus, he saluted Him and said he was sorry and that it was the wrong door. Even though Jesus told the devil to come in for it was the right door he politely apologized again, insisted that it was the wrong door, and did not enter. In the same way, most Christians have only received Jesus as a visitor in their lives without asking him to take control. This is why Satan comes into their lives all the time to beat them up. If you are one of those people who are suffering everyday at the hands of the Devil, why wait. Once Jesus is right beside you, ask him to be in charge like the woman. The next time Satan knocks your door, Jesus will be there to open it - and guess what will happen.

The disciples' second crisis

The disciples faced a second crisis after the one with the storm. When they came out of the boat they were confronted with two demon-possessed men who the Bible describes as so violent that no-one could pass that way. However because Jesus the problem-solver was present, He dealt with the situation by casting out the demons from the men as recorded in Matthew 8:28-33. "When he arrived at the other side in the region of the Gadarenes, two demon-possessed men coming from the tombs met him. They were so violent that no-one could pass that way. "What do you want with us, Son of God?" they shouted. "Have you come here to torture us before the appointed time?" Some distance from them, a large herd of pigs was feeding. The demons begged Jesus, "If you drive us out, send us into the herd of pigs." He said to them, "Go!" So they came out and went into the pigs, and the whole herd rushed down the steep bank into the lake and died in the water. Those tending the pigs ran off, went into the town and reported all this, including what had happened to the demon-possessed men."

Earlier in Joseph' story in Genesis 39, we see that there was a time when everything was going well for him in Egypt. It seemed his trouble was over because he was put in charge of everything to do with matters in master's house. This was when the Devil using his master's wife tempted him and this resulted in him being imprisoned, but thank God in the prison too the Bible says 'God was with him' and so he got promoted even in the prison. "When his master heard the story his wife told him, saying, "This is how your slave treated me," he burned with anger. Joseph's master took him and put him in prison, the place where the king's prisoners were confined. But while Joseph was there in the prison, the LORD was with him; he showed him kindness and granted him favour in the eyes of the prison warder. So the warder put Joseph in charge of all those held in the prison, and he was made responsible for all that was done there. The warder paid no attention to anything under Joseph's care, because the Lord was with Joseph and gave him success in whatever he did." Genesis 39:19-23

There is a very interesting point in the second crisis stories about the disciples and that of Joseph's. It is more evidence that the devil never gives up on anybody no matter who you are, what you have or your state. You may be in a state of false security thinking that you have made it, then the devil will strike when you least expect him to. This is why believers must be vigilant at all times. Jesus said in Matthew 12:43-45, "When an evil spirit comes out of a man, it goes through arid places seeking rest and does not find it. Then it says, 'I will return to the house I left.' When it arrives, it finds the house unoccupied, swept clean and put in order. Then it goes and takes with it seven other spirits more wicked than itself, and they go in and live there. And the final condition of that man is worse than the first. That is how it will be with this wicked generation."

Sometimes we may face crisis after crisis and it seems that you get out of one problem and another one emerges. You got a job and when it looked safe, it's gone. You lost a man or woman then it seems like you had found fulfillment in a new one, but as time goes on, it transpires that the new one is much worse than the previous. Do not despair as there's good news and more encouragement for those who will stay loyal to God. It does not matter how many times the Devil approaches you, as long as you are connected and loyal to God He will remain faithful to you, promotion and success will follow (in any matter). The Bible says that though the enemy will come like a flood, the Spirit of the Lord will raise its standard against it. So, you must be strong and courageous as the Lord told Joshua in Joshua 1:6, 7 and 9, "Be strong and courageous, because you will lead these people to inherit the land I swore to their forefathers to give them. Be strong and very courageous. Be careful to obey all the law my servant Moses gave you; do not turn from it to the right or to the left, that you may be successful wherever you go. Do not let this Book of the Law depart from your mouth; meditate on it day and night, so that you may be careful to do everything written in it. Then you will be prosperous and successful. "Have I not commanded you? Be strong and courageous. Do not be terrified; do not be discouraged, for the

Lord your God will be with you wherever you go." Joshua 1:6-9

The Lord promised to be with Joshua just as he was with Moses. This was when he was asked to lead the Israelites to the Promised Land after the death of Moses. The quotations above means that Joshua had to be conscious at all times that the Lord is with him; he had to be reassured that he was not alone. Therefore, anything he did or any battle he fought he was physically powerful and brave knowing that the Lord was with him. In other words, he was connected to God.

Elisha: Elisha also is an excellent example of what it means to be truly focused, he demonstrated this when he focused on his master Elijah until the day he was taken to heaven by God. He did not allow anything to distract him and received a double portion of anointing. In 2 Kings 2:9-13 (NKJV) the Scripture says: "And so it was, when they had crossed over, that Elijah said to Elisha, "Ask! What may I do for you, before I am taken away from you?" Elisha said, "Please let a double portion of your spirit be upon me." So he said, You have asked a hard thing. Nevertheless, if you see me when I am taken from you, it shall be so for you; but if not, it shall not be so." Then it happened, as they continued on and talked, that suddenly a chariot of fire appeared with horses of fire, and separated the two of them; and Elijah went up by a whirlwind into heaven. And Elisha saw it, and he cried out, "My father, my father, the chariot of Israel and its horsemen!" So he saw him no more. And he took hold of his own clothes and tore them into two pieces. He also took up the mantle of Elijah that had fallen from him, and went back and stood by the bank of the Jordan".

This account of Elisha and Elijah also shows that when you focus on Jesus Christ and rely on Him, this will generate great loyalty towards him. Elisha was committed to his master and ready to serve him to the last minute. He did not allow what he heard from a group of prophets or even a series of persuasions from Elijah his master to stop him from being devoted to him. Elisha kept the word of Elijah his master that he said to him in 2 King 2:10 "….if you see me when I am taken from you, it shall be so for you; but if not, it shall not be so." He received his heart's desire in verse 12 as he kept the word. As I conclude this part of the book, I encourage you with the words or the story of these two prophets and also remind you of a song I always sing whenever I preach about being focused on Christ. It goes like this:

"Believer let your eyes be on Christ
Halleluiah keep looking at Him
Stop talking and grumbling
For he can easily change the sky
The Lord will keep and make you prosper"

In short, the message this song projects is 'keeping your eyes on Jesus guarantees you peace and success as a believer'

Causes And Effects Of Failure To Focus On Christ

Nothing happens without a cause; there is a cause for everything. It is also true that every cause has an effect. Everybody would like good things happen to them but good things do not happen all the time. There are some reasons for this. Below are some of the reasons why some people fail to focus on Christ even though it is guaranteed success to focus on Him. This applies to those who are disconnected from Christ, the Vine. We live in a world today where more than ever, the Devil has all that it takes to distract people's attention away from Christ. He uses these things to cause fear and panic, anger, discouragements, selfish ambitions etc, because of these senses of the flesh most people are impatient, unable to wait on God's timing. Let us refer back to our foundation Scripture for this sub-title 'Focus on Christ'. In Hebrew 12:1, we saw that the writer advices that believers should run with patience. This means that to be able to focus on Christ you need patience.

Causes:

One of the major things the devil uses to distract the attention of believers and unbelievers alike from Jesus is the flesh. This is why people refuse to focus on Christ and are in love with the things of the world. In other words, the desire for the things of the world which is connected to the five senses of the flesh or the works of the flesh. These works of the flesh are caused by lack of control of the five bodily senses as stated in Galatians 5:19–21. These things are:

What we see with our eyes: What you see with your eyes can weaken the defenses of your mind. In other words, it can cause great fear to come upon you. In 1 Samuel chapter 17 it is recorded that King Saul and his army were broken by fear because they saw Goliath as a giant so none of them could fight. The Bible describes him in (verse 4-7) and the words of his mouth and states that it terrified the Israelites; they were deeply shaken when they heard him speak. He even defied the God of Israel as stated in verse 8-11 because they had forgotten their God. On the other hand, David, a young boy who was connected to God and whose eyes were on Him saw Goliath as an uncircumcised Philistine and a pagan who had no covenant with God. David also saw him as one who had no protection from the Lord so he told King Saul to inform the armies of Israel, in verse 32 of the same chapter, "Let no-one lose heart on account of this Philistine; your servant will go and fight him".

King Saul wanted to stop David from carrying out his intention because of what he knew Goliath could do as a fighter. However, David insisted he could do it because his eyes were on God as stated in verse 33. He further demonstrated his dependence on God when he met Goliath as is seen in verses 45-47. David said to the Philistine, "You come against me with sword and spear and javelin, but I come against you in the name of the Lord Almighty, the God of the armies of Israel, whom you have defied. This day the Lord will hand you over to me, and I'll strike you down and cut off your head. Today I will give the carcasses of the Philistine army to the birds of the air and the beasts of the earth, and the whole world will know that there is a God in Israel. All those gathered here will know that it is not by sword or spear that the Lord saves; for the battle is the Lord's, and he will give all of you into our hands". The next verses records that David killed Goliath with only one of the five stones he had in his hand because he relied on God. It is clear that that King Saul and his men were defeated even before the fight began because they depended on the arms of the flesh but not on God.

In another incident, ten out of twelve spies who were sent by Moses to spy out the Promised Land came back with a very bad report because of what they saw. They like Saul and his men depended on the arm of the flesh. This is the report they gave to Moses: "We went into the land to which you sent us, and it does flow with milk and honey! Here is its fruit. But the people who live there are powerful and the cities are fortified and very large. We even saw descendants of Anak there.

The Amalekites live in the Negev; the Hittites, Jebusites and Amorites live in the hill country; and the Canaanites live near the sea and along the Jordan. "Then Caleb silenced the people before Moses and said, "We should go up and take possession of the land, for we can certainly do it. "But the men who had gone up with him said, "We can't attack those people; they are stronger than we are. "And they spread among the Israelites a bad report about the land they had explored. They said, "The land we explored devours those living in it. All the people we saw there are of great size. We saw the Nephilim there (the descendants of Anak come from the Nephilim). We seemed like grasshoppers in our own eyes, and we looked the same to them." Numbers 13:27-33

Do you know that what you see can affect your whole life? Do you know what it can do to you? Numbers 14:6-8 says, "The ten spies forgot the Lord - who had promised them the Promised Land - because of what they saw." In other words, they were disconnected from the Lord because of fear. However Joshua and Caleb held on to God's promise and gave a positive report. Joshua the son of Nun and Caleb son of Jephunneh, who were among those who had explored the land, tore their clothes and said to the entire Israelite assembly, "The land we passed through and explored is exceedingly good. If the Lord is pleased with us, he will lead us into that land, a land flowing with milk and honey, and will give it to us."

Their bad report, which came from what they saw, resulted in all of the ten spies dying in the wilderness without seeing the Promised Land. Of the twelve spies, only Joshua and Caleb got there because they stayed connected to God through His promise. I want to use the above story to advice you not to go by what you see; it will disconnect you from God and the Devil could use that to deceive you. You could also lose your Promised Land; instead you should be led by the Spirit of God which is to have faith in Him. The Scripture commanded believers not to be moved by sight as stated in 2 Corinthians 5:17.

What we hear with our ears: The Ears are another tool of distraction and loss of faith. They are one of the distractive tools used by the Devil to cause people to take their eyes off Jesus. Those who always want to hear things, (especially that which is negative) will always have problems keeping their eyes on Jesus. The ear is also one of the enemy's tools to distract people's attention from Christ. Jesus knew the effect of what the Devil can do through the ears; so he asked Jairus not to worry about what people say but keep his faith. That means to keep his eyes on him and stay connected to Him. In Mark 5:35-42 the Scripture it states: "While Jesus was still speaking; some men came from the house of Jairus, the synagogue ruler."Your daughter is dead," they said. "Why bother the teacher anymore?" Ignoring what they said, Jesus told the synagogue ruler, "Don't be afraid; just believe." He did not let anyone follow him except Peter, James and John the brother of James. When they came to the home of the synagogue ruler, Jesus saw a commotion, with people crying and wailing loudly. He went in and said to them, "Why all this commotion and wailing? The child is not dead but asleep." But they laughed at him. After he put them all out, he took the child's father and mother and the disciples who were with him, and went in where the child was. He took her by the hand and said to her, "Talitha koum!" (which means, "Little girl, I say to you, get up!"). Immediately the girl stood up and walked around (she was twelve years old). At this they were completely astonished".

Listening to others is one of ways the Devil uses to distract people's attention from Jesus. Therefore, if you want to keep your focus on him, be careful of the things you listen to. Those who do not want to see your progress or happiness will tell you things to discourage or frighten you. These things will definitely stop you from moving forward. You can see from the above Scriptures, Mark 5:35-42 that after connecting himself to Jesus, who could help save his daughter, the Devil wanted to use some men in his house to bring him bad report about her death. But when the synagogue ruler took note under Jesus' instruction, he brought her back to life; I believe without doubt that the news of her death would cause him a great panic. Stay connected to him and do not be carried away by what you hear. And whatever is dead in your life will return back to life in Jesus name. With him, you can resist any fear, panic, anger, and discouragement.

Another story in Mark 10:46-52 is about the blind man Bartimaeus who received his sight.

This happened because he did not allow people who told him to stop pursuing his heart's desire to control him as he had set his eyes on Jesus. Firstly, as his eyes were on him he also had faith that Jesus was able to heal him. Secondly Bartimaeus was looking to Jesus for his healing; he did not blame anyone unlike the man at the pool of Bethesda. Not even those who were telling him to shut up, they couldn't convince him as he shouted the more when Jesus asked him: "What do you want me to do for you?" He was able to say, "Rabbi, I want to see" without hesitation. Do not listen to what people are saying about you they will distract you from pursuing your God given ambition. Shut your ears and keep your eyes on him to keep the hope of your dream alive. This is the reason why we must be very careful of what we tell others. Your words can bring encouragement to someone that will help him to do better even if he has no courage and believe to do so. On the other hand, what you tell someone can also bring discouragement to them which could destroy their morals and this could affect their effort to do better.

In Colossians 3:21, when Paul was giving instructions for Christian households on how to live, he advised parents not to discourage their children. He said: "Fathers, do not embitter your children, or they will become discouraged."

NLT puts it this way: "Father's don't aggravate your children. If you do, they will become discouraged and quit trying." In the context of Paul's instruction, I am also advising you to be careful about what you tell your children. Because you could discourage them and that will cause them to stop trying or moving forward.

What we taste with our tongue or mouth: The whole human race fell and died spiritually because of Eve. The mother of all human races saw and tasted of the forbidden fruit when she was deceived by the serpent, more about this will be dealt with later in the book.

And what we touch or feel with our hand: Similarly if a person is depending on outward things or human abilities, he is being controlled by the flesh which can distract him from Christ. Paul said "For those who live according to the flesh set their minds on the things of the flesh, but those who live according to the Spirit, the things of the Spirit. For to be carnally minded is death, but to be spiritually minded is life and peace." - Romans 8:5-6 (NKJV)

More about the love of the world

The Scripture talk refers to three types of the world:

1. The universe or the earth
2. Things in the world, the pleasures in the world
3. The people or the inhabitants of the world

In the context of this message, "Focus on Christ" in this part of the book we will only consider the second; things in the world, or the pleasures in the world which is relevant to us this time. The love for the things or the pleasures of this world will take your eye off Christ Jesus. In His advice to the people to store their treasures in heaven, he said in Matthew 6:24, "No-one can serve two masters. Either he will hate the one and love the other, or he will be devoted to the one and despise the other. You cannot serve both God and Money."

Matthew 16:26 (NLT), "And how do you benefit if you gain the whole world but lose your own soul in the process? Is anything worth more than your soul?

Matthew 4:8-9 (NLT), "Next the Devil took him to the peak of a very high mountain and showed him the nations of the world and all their glory. Fright "I will give it all to you," he said, "if you will only kneel down and worship me."

1 John 2:15-17, "Do not love the world or anything in the world. If anyone loves the world, the love of the Father is not in him. For everything in the world—the cravings of sinful man, the lust of his eyes and the boasting of what he has and does—comes not from the Father but from the world. The world and its desires pass away, but the man who does the will of God lives forever."

As emphasized earlier, one of the greatest enticements of the devil is to lure Christians to take their eyes off Christ. This happens through focusing on the things of the world, therefore

Christians must be very careful how they chase these things. The Devil can easily lure you into his kingdom just as he tried with Jesus Christ. He must be the primary focus of Christians whilst all other things become secondary. (Matthew 6:33)

One day a fox went out looking for food but found nothing. On its way back home to his amazement, he saw a crow with meat in its beak in a tree. Immediately he decided to do something that would cause the bird to drop the meat from its mouth, but no amount of trickery could persuade the crow to open its mouth. So finally, he said to the crow, "Among all the other things I fancy about you. It's your chirping I fancy the most." The crow was very flattered by this and opened its mouth to show Mr. Fox how nice its chirp was. The meat dropped out of its mouth and landed at the feet of Mr. Fox who grabbed it quickly and fled.

In another story that one day the King of the Jungle called for a race between the tortoise and the dog. He promised to offer his daughter as a prize in marriage to the winner. In this story too, the tortoise' guess was as good as anybody in the jungle. He knew he had lost the race in advance because he could not race against the dog and win unless he comes out with a plan. The tortoise then acted on the advice of some elders of the jungle. He got himself some bones from the local butcher and put them alongside the tracks before the race started. The time came and both the dog and the tortoise came to the starting line and the whistle went for them to start. As expected, the dog was quickly out in front while the tortoise slowly plodded along, suddenly, the dog saw the bones along the tracks and unable to resist the temptation posed by the bones, one by one he began eating them. This gave the tortoise the chance to go past him and finish the race as the surprise winner with the most precious prize in the jungle, the - daughter of the king of the jungle. The dog lost the race because he lost sight of the winning prize to the temptation of bones.

In the same way, some believers are like the crow and lose their meat to the devil, the fox, others like the dog lose the race set before them. The writer of the book of Hebrews warns about many things that hinders and the sin that so easily entangle you. Yes, there may be obstacles in the way but if you keep your eyes on Him, He will always keep you until you win the race.

Traditions

Traditions, which is the belief, custom, principle or standard passed on from generations to generations is also another cause of people unable to focus on Christ or stay connected to Him. This was one of the reasons why the Pharisees and the Scribes could not believe in Jesus because they were too familiar with the traditions of the elders more than the word of God. Matthew records one of such incidents in Matthew 15:1-6 (NKJV), "Then the scribes and Pharisees who were from Jerusalem came to Jesus, saying, "Why do Your disciples transgress the tradition of the elders? For they do not wash their hands when they eat bread." He answered and said to them, "Why do you also transgress the commandment of God because of your tradition? For God commanded, saying, *'Honour your father and your mother'; and, 'He who curses father or mother, let him be put to death.'* But you say, 'Whoever says to his father or mother, "Whatever profit you might have received from me is a gift to God" then he need not honour his father or mother.' Thus you have made the commandment of God of no effect by your tradition."

You can see from the above story that traditions are also the cause of people losing their focus on Christ. The reason for this is that traditions focus more on the laws and actions of men, and not God's, i.e. faith in Christ and his saving work. Therefore I advice that if you want to stay connected to Christ or to focus on Him, you must be careful how you rate and hold on to traditions.

Some of the effects of failure to focus on Christ: Like the unproductive branches in John 15, there is definitely a major consequence for all those who fail to focus on Christ. The following are a few, which I want, discuss with you:

1. **Sinking or drowning in circumstances:** The following story in Mathew 14:25-30 is a fitting example to this fact where Peter began to sink in front of Jesus on the water because he took his eyes off Jesus. He was looking at the mighty wind of the sea when he heard the sound.

"During the fourth watch of the night Jesus went out to them, walking on the lake. When the disciples saw him walking on the lake, they were terrified. "It's a ghost," they said, and cried out in fear. But Jesus immediately said to them: "Take courage! It is I. Don't be afraid." "Lord, if it's you," Peter replied, "tell me to come to you on the water." "Come," he said. Then Peter got down out of the boat, walked on the water and came towards Jesus. But when he saw the wind, he was afraid and, beginning to sink, cried out, "Lord, save me!"

Quite often, people are surprised by Peter's behavior in the story above, and would criticize him for his actions. They will ask a question like, "How could he take his eyes off of Jesus that was the result of his sinking?" What many people don't know is that there are many ways in which we also take our eyes off of Jesus. Just like Peter, anyone who takes his eyes off Jesus loses concentration or focus on him. These individuals have no faith in him and therefore loses grip of life. They become overwhelmed with problems or other circumstances. As I said before - in our world today, there are problems everywhere, and it will only take concentration and focus on Jesus to survive. Therefore, I am advising you what to do in all circumstances - keep your eyes on him and you will stay afloat. Those who fail to focus on Christ are usually overtaken by problems, which can be easily seen on their faces, their appearances and the way they speak.

2. **Complaining and blaming people:** Focusing on people and problems or physical things always results in complaining and blaming people. Christianity is supposed to be Christ-focused as mentioned earlier. However, there are many people who go to church and called themselves Christians but are not Christ-focused. This has been the reason for so many problems faced by many believers in the church today. Just like the man at the pool of Bethesda, these Christians focus on people and problems because they have taken their eyes off Christ. In the story of the man at the pool of Bethesda in John 5:1-9 we see that:

1. Even though he was at the right place, he had a wrong frame of mind; his focus was not on Jesus the Son of God who has power to do all things
2. He did not recognize Jesus the healer
3. He did not recognize Jesus and so he was giving him wrong answers when asked simple questions
4. He blamed others for his inability to get into the pool

There are those who lose focus on Christ and concentrate on people and problems, then complain and blame people for their failure. Focus your eyes on Jesus and you will stop complaining and blaming people. The man at the pool of Bethesda had his focus on his problem and people. In fact, he did not know who Jesus was at all because of where he placed his focus that was the reason for his wrong answer to a simple question.

In the same way, so many people today have lost focus on Christ and are focusing on healing rather than the healer, deliverance instead of the deliverer. There are those in the churches today who are without Christ. They have not been born again because they are there not for Christ but for personal interest. Is Christ your focus? Do you rely or depend on him? David said "I have set the Lord always before me; Because, He is at my right hand I shall not be moved" - Psalms 16:8 (NKJV). Why do you go to Church is it because of Christ, anybody else or anything?

Many are like the man at the pool of Bathsheba, in the right place (the church) but are missing the benefits of being a Christian. They are in the wrong frame of mind and their focus is not on Christ. Note that whenever you lose Christ as your focus, people and problems become your focus; and like this man at the pool, when people become your focus you always rely on them for help. Since men are limited and cannot help or respond to you at all the times, you will always have problems with them when they fail you. Focus on Christ who is always able and available to come to your aid at any time no matter where you are. If you rely on Him, he will send someone to help you whenever you need it. The worse part of it is that when some people notice that you rely on them they become proud and in most cases, mistreat you. They think that without them you cannot live or make it. I personally had friends and people who I gave a lot of respect because of the help they gave me. Unfortunately, these people later thought I was weak and foolish and that without them I could not do anything. Some mistreated me and others become disrespectful to me but thank God (who is my focus) I believe without any doubt these individuals have heard or will hear that God has elevated me without them. As you read this book I advise you to keep your eyes on Jesus, put all your hope in Him to let Him know that you cannot live or make it without Him. He will use His mercy and faithfulness and supply all your needs according to His riches in glory. Men and women will fail and disappoint you when you need them most, however God will always answer your call immediately. Even if there is a delay, it will be in your interest, for the Lord is never too early or too late but is always on time. Praise God!

Again, I want you to note that when you lose focus on Christ, you lose hope and then you begin to complain and start to blame others for your inadequacy. You do not need anybody to succeed or make it in life; you need Christ. One way to identify those who have lost focus on Christ is through their confessions; there is too much complaining and the blaming of others. Those whose eyes are on Jesus will leave all things in His hands and don't spend time complaining and blaming others; they trust Jesus being in control and know all will be well. David showed the importance of trusting God instead of men when He warned us in Psalms 146:3-10. He said that because men are mortal beings, we must not put our trust in them as they can die at any time destroying any plans that they may have with or for you. David said God is the only one who remains faithful forever. When you trust Him, you will never be disappointed as when dealing with men.

3. **Loss of faith:** Without Christ as your focus, there is no faith. Remember, He is the author and finisher of our faith. Hebrews 12:2, our foundation scripture for this sub-heading "Focus on Christ" states that He is the foundation of all who believe in God. Without Him, there would not be salvation for no one or Christianity for that matter. Christ is the object of our faith. When you lose him as your focus, you lose what it takes to survive as the Scripture says 'the just shall live by faith' (Habakkuk 2:4; Romans 1:17; Galatians 3:11; Hebrews 10:38). When you lose faith in Him, everything collapses because you have lost connection with God the Gardener. The Bible says, "And without faith it is impossible to please God, because anyone who comes to him must believe that he exists and that he rewards those who earnestly seek him." Hebrews 11:6

It is important to remember that without him we can do nothing. He said in John 15:5 that we cannot solve any problem ourselves and we cannot fight the Devil on our own. The Devil makes us think we can do it on our own and even faster. There are cases where some Christians leave the church in times of overwhelming problems. When you ask why, they will tell you they left in order to solve their problems. Now, ask me how many of these people have been able to solve any problem on their own? None.

4. **Disrespect and disloyal:** So many believers have no respect for Christ and so are not committed to Him, even though they call themselves Christians and may go to church every Sunday. When a person goes to Church every day, but loses focus on Christ; then he or she has also lost respect for Him. In my mind, he or she has also become disloyal and has no respect for Jesus or God. These are the people who don't fear God and don't fear sin, even though they may call themselves Christians. These people don't even care

what they do in the house of God. Even though they are in the church every day, their eyes are not on Christ, so they live their lives to please themselves. They do not really care if what they are doing brings shame to Christ. Christ refers to these people as the ones who just pay lip service, he said, "These people draw near to Me with their mouth, And honour Me with their lips, But their heart is far from Me." Matthew 15:8 (NKJV). They are not prepared to live according to God's commandments; they only want to, live according to what pleases them, whether it is right or wrong. These people have received Christ as their saviour but he is not their Lord. This means that they take no instructions from him. They would lie, gossip, backbite, and even fornicate in the house of God. They claim to be Christians but Christ is not in them, they have no intimate relationship with Christ. These said people enjoy sin because they do not possess the Holy Spirit so there is no conviction in them. Jesus said when the Spirit comes, He will convict the world of sin. When Christ is your focus you are led by the Holy Spirit.

5. **Friend of the Devil and enemy to the Church:** When a person loses focus on Christ becoming disrespectful and disloyal to Christ, he also becomes a friend of the Devil and enemy to Christ and the Church (the body of Christ). This person has now become a tool for the Devil against the church. In most cases, the Devil lets them think they are more righteous than anybody, even better than their Pastor and the leaders of the church they attend. In other cases, more often than not, some split churches and form another church and destroy the work of God which has taken so many years to build. Some are not aware they are working for the Devil, and worst of all justify their actions by denigrating the church, Pastors and other leaders. This is all down to the fact that when Christ is no longer the focus you become infected with the insecurity syndrome. For more details on insecurity syndrome read my next book about insecurity.

6. **Destruction:** There is an equally important danger from losing Christ as the focus. Whenever this happens, the person affected becomes proud as he depends on his own ability and credits himself for all of his achievements. According to scripture, this result only brings destruction. Solomon said, "Pride goes before destruction, a haughty spirit before a fall." Proverbs 16:18

Again, he said "Before his downfall a man's heart is proud, but humility comes before honour" Proverbs 18:12

Peter also said when he advised young men, "Young men, in the same way be submissive to those who are older. All of you, clothe yourselves with humility towards one another, because, "God opposes the proud but gives grace to the humble." Humble yourselves, therefore, under God's mighty hand, that he may lift you up in due time. Cast all your anxiety on him because he cares for you." 1 Peter 5:5-7

God humbled King Nebuchadnezzar when he exalted himself. "All this happened to King Nebuchadnezzar. Twelve months later, as the king was walking on the roof of the royal palace of Babylon, he said, "Is not this the great Babylon I have built as the royal residence, by my mighty power and for the glory of my majesty?" The words were still on his lips when a voice came from heaven, "This is what is decreed for you, King Nebuchadnezzar: Your royal authority has been taken from you. You will be driven away from people and will live with the wild animals; you will eat grass like cattle. Seven times will pass by for you until you acknowledge that the Most High is sovereign over the kingdoms of men and gives them to anyone he wishes." Immediately what had been said about Nebuchadnezzar was fulfilled. He was driven away from people and ate grass like cattle. His body was drenched with the dew of heaven until his hair grew like the feathers of an eagle and his nails like the claws of a bird." Daniel 4:28-33

What happened to Nebuchadnezzar could happen to anyone as God is faithful; He is the respecter of no persons, whatever He says comes to pass and there is no favoritism in Him. In Luke 12:16-21, Jesus told his disciples of a parable about a rich foolish man who did not have his eyes on Jesus. The man thought that he had earned all his wealth through his own ability so he was proud and boasted, because of the man's arrogance the Lord took away his life. Therefore, it is important that you do not take your example from a foolish rich man, never take your eyes off God, lest you give way to pride and God will oppose you. Focus, concentrate and acknowledge him; give him credit for all that you are and he will lift you up in due time. Anyone who loses focus on Christ and becomes proud is in danger of heading to destruction. "Keep your eyes on him no matter what happens" never allow anything or anybody to detract your attention from Him. If anything or anybody successfully distracts you to take your eyes from Christ, he, she or it was able to become the greatest influence in your life.

Remember in the story of the King of the jungle, the dog lost the most precious thing in the jungle because the tortoise succeeded in distracting him with bones. Take heed of the crow, which lost its meat because of the flattering words of the fox. We live in the world today and this end time, wisdom has abounded. There are men and women being used by the Devil even in the house of God who promise you everything if you give yourself to them. In other words, they want to lure you to take your eyes off God. In extreme cases, a man can promise a married woman much more than her husband if she yields to his demands. Similarly, a woman can promise a married man that she could be more caring and helpful than his own wife. In such instances, your eyes must be focused on Jesus (our defensive weapon, the sword of the Spirit, which is the word of God) to defeat the Devil. Jesus Christ demonstrated this when he was tempted by the Devil. Matthew 4:8-10 states: "Again, the devil took him to a very high mountain and showed him all the kingdoms of the world and their splendour. "All this I will give you," he said, "if you will bow down and worship me." Jesus said to him, "Away from me, Satan! For it is written, 'Worship the Lord your God, and serve him only.'"

Those Who Wait Upon The Lord

"He gives power to the weak, And to those who have no might He increases strength. Even the youths shall faint and be weary, And the young men shall utterly fall, But those who wait on the Lord Shall renew their strength; They shall mount up with wings like eagles, They shall run and not be weary, They shall walk and not faint." Isaiah 40:29-31 (NKJV)

Background of the story: In the first thirty nine chapters of the book of Isaiah the prophet calls on the people to repent of their sins, otherwise the destruction of the Lord will befall on them. The last twenty-seven chapters (40-66) are words of consolation and hope as the prophet unfolds God's promise of future blessings through the Messiah. Chapter forty is the centre of this book which emphasizes that for the people to be confident in God, he had to remind them and all believers about who He is and what He is capable of. Furthermore, it also highlights what he can do for His children and for those who wait on Him. He ended the chapter with the opening Scripture for this part of the book, by relating Himself to what is more familiar to the people - what they will be if they will wait upon Him. In verse 31, the Amplified version says, "But those who wait for the Lord [who expect, look for, and hope in Him] shall change and renew their strength and power: they shall lift their wings and mount up [close to God] as eagles [mount up to the sun]: they shall run and not weary, they shall walk and not faint or become tired".

It is clear from that quotation what the Scripture is stating. Those who *wait* upon the Lord will be strong like an eagle and in the context of this book, those who remain in the Vine which means to stay connected to the Lord. In this part of the book, 'Stay Connected to Christ' I would like to look at the characteristics of an eagle, to explain the message the Lord is telling His children who will abide in Him, wait upon Him, or those who will depend on Him.

The Eagle as we know it is: a large beautiful bird of prey (one that attacks and eats other birds and small animals, etc) It has superb sight and is very strong.

Eagles are noted for:
Size – very big or huge
Strength – power or might
Powers of flight – can fly at great height
Vision – have far seeing sight – Visionary, dream or revelation

This means that those who wait upon the Lord like an eagle will be:

Very huge or big in size: God is immeasurable; no one knows his height, length or breadth. This reminds me of a song - God is bigger than anything.

Bigger than all the shadows that fall across my path, God is bigger than any mountain that I can or cannot see. He's bigger than all the confusion, bigger than anything; God is bigger than any mountain that I can or cannot see.

Chorus: He's bigger than all my problems, bigger than all my fears; God is bigger than any mountain that I can or cannot see. Oh, yes, he's bigger than all my questions, bigger than anything; God is bigger than any mountain that I can or cannot see.

He's bigger than all the giants of pain and unbelief; God is bigger than any mountain that I can or cannot see. He's bigger than any discouragement, bigger than anything; My God is bigger than any mountain that I can or cannot see.

The message is clear and that is, those who wait upon the Lord will be bigger than anything or anybody as God is. The eagle represents and symbolizes God in this context. All things become small to those who look to God. Those who wait on Jesus are secured or saved because He has never lost a fight. The Akans from Ghana will say: "when you hide behind an elephant you will never be hit by a bullet". Because of its size it is able to absorb any bullet from any direction. Similarly, a hen will always protect its little chicks when they run to take cover under its wings, when they catch sight of a hawk, which is their greatest enemy. In the same way God is able to cover those who depend on Him at all times from any danger. The writer of Psalm 91 gives so much comfort to those who dwell in the secret place of the Most High God and in the context of this part of the book those who wait upon the Lord.

Powerful in strength, the second characteristic of an eagle: The eagle's description informs us that because of its power and strength it is able to attack or eat other birds and some animals. In this message the prophet is portraying that God is powerful in strength. One of the attributes of God is that He is Omnipotent, which means all powerful - the God Almighty. This attribute reveals Him as one who has the ultimate power and capability to do whatever he wants to do without anybody or anything being able to stop Him. The eagle soars high above reaching awesome heights because of his strength and wingspan. God is beyond everything or everybody, He is able to do everything without measure anytime and anywhere, His power is unlimited, nothing is too hard for him as Jeremiah said, "Ah, Sovereign Lord, you have made the heavens and the earth by your great power and outstretched arm. Nothing is too hard for you," Jeremiah 32:17.

Then the word of the Lord came to Jeremiah: "I am the Lord, the God of all mankind. Is anything too hard for me?" Jeremiah 32:26-27. The idea of God's omnipotence finds expression in the name El-Shaddai when he proved Himself to Abraham in Genesis 18. He pledged to fulfill his promised to him "Is anything too hard for the Lord? I will return to you at the appointed time next year and Sarah will have a son," Genesis 18:14.

God's power was revealed again when He led the Israelites through the Red sea on dry land; the sea covered the Egyptian soldiers as expressed in the song of Moses and the children of Israel in Exodus14-15:1-19. Job also expresses God's omnipotence when he said, "If He takes away, who can hinder him? Who can say to him, what are you doing?" Job 9:12. What situation do you face? What state do you find yourself in now? Similar to Lazarus' sisters, you may think that your situation is so deplorable that there is no life. The good news is Jesus is the resurrection, the life, and those who believe in him will also live; just believe and do not limit him and he will inject life into your situation.

"When Martha heard that Jesus was coming, she went out to meet him, but Mary stayed at home."Lord," Martha said to Jesus, "if you had been here, my brother would not have died. But I know that even now God will give you whatever you ask." Jesus said to her, "Your brother will rise again." Martha answered, "I know he will rise again in the resurrection at the last day." Jesus said to her, "I am the resurrection and the life. He who believes in me will live, even though he dies; and whoever lives and believes in me will never die. Do you believe this?" John 11:19-26

"Jesus, once more deeply moved, came to the tomb. It was a cave with a stone laid across the entrance. "Take away the stone," he said. "But, Lord," said Martha, the sister of the dead man, "by this time there is a bad odour, for he has been there four days." Then Jesus said, "Did I not tell you that if you believed, you would see the glory of God?" So they took away the stone. Then Jesus looked up and said, "Father, I thank you that you have heard me. I knew that you always hear me, but I said this for the benefit of the people standing here, that they may believe that you sent me." When he had said this, Jesus called in a loud voice, "Lazarus, come out!" The dead man came out, his hands and feet wrapped with strips of linen, and a cloth around his face. Jesus said to them, "Take off the grave clothes and let him go." John 11:38-44

Since the eagle is powerful in strength, its presence brings panic and frightens other birds and animals. Acts of God, cause awe and panic amongst people and even the demons become scared. James said, "You believe that there is one God. You do well. Even the demons believe--and tremble!" James 2:19 (NKJV). The Lord is powerful in strength that is why He is able to renew the strength of those who wait upon Him.

The eagle exerts its strength through its mouth or beak and through the legs by holding on to things firmly. In the same way, God is able to hold in His hands firmly all those who wait upon Him. Responding to the Jews demand "if you are the Christ, tell us plainly" Jesus answered them, "I told you, and you do not believe. The works that I do in My Father's name, they bear witness of Me. But you do not believe, because you are not of My sheep, as I said to you. My sheep hear My voice, and I know them, and they follow Me. And I give them eternal life, and they shall never perish; neither shall anyone snatch them out of My hand. My Father, who has given them to Me, is greater than all; and no one is able to snatch them out of My Father's hand." John 10:26-29 (NKJV)

The message to you is that be assured that since you wait or depend on God, you are saved and well protected; nothing or nobody can snatch you out of God's hand.

Powerful in flight: The Amplified version of the Bible says those who wait on God shall lift their wings and mount up [close to God] as eagles [mount up to the sun]. This means that these people can 'fly' very high, just as an eagle can soar higher in the sky than any other bird. In my view, this means that those who wait upon the Lord will rise above any challenge or circumstances in life. No problem can overtake them; they are always on top. Peter walked on the sea when his eyes were on Jesus. Someone said, because he was looking to Jesus, he walked on His word which told him to come. 'And Peter answered Him and said, "Lord, if it is You, command me to come to You on the water." So He said, "Come." And when Peter had come down out of the boat, he walked on the water to go to Jesus.' Matthew 14:28-29 (NKJV)

Similar to Peter you can also live above any circumstances irrespective of how dangerous it may be. If Jesus Christ is your focus, as long as you truly rely on him. Then there is no problem that will be beyond; by His grace, you will be able to overcome them. In our world today, more than ever before, there is so much that believers come up against, it is enough to make them lose heart and go weary. Yet, in spite of that, believers will still fly as high as eagles to survive any test.

Vision (Good sight): Relating this to those who will wait upon the Lord, this means these people will be a visionary. They will have dreams or revelations; nothing will hinder them because they will be seeing from a far distance. One of God's attributes is that He is Omniscient, He is all-knowing, i.e. He knows everything, past, present, and future. He is infinite in knowledge and nothing is hidden from him. Every detail about all things is open to him (Psalm 139:1-6). His knowledge is perfect. (Job 37:16) He knows the inner heart of men (1 Samuel 16:7; 1 Chronicles 28:9). He even knows the number of our hair (Matthew 10:30; Hebrews 4:13). In Matthew 1:19-21, God revealed this attribute when he saw Joseph, Mary's husband's heart when he had secretly decided to put away Mary because she was pregnant even though he was yet to go bed with her. Every detail of our lives is before him. He knows when we are happy and when we are sad and knows whatever we do. Similar to Jonah no one can run from him. "The word of the Lord came to Jonah son of Amittai: "Go to the great city of Nineveh and preach against it, because its wickedness has come up before me." But Jonah ran away from the Lord and headed for Tarshish. He went down to Joppa, where he found a ship bound for that port. After paying the fare, he went aboard and sailed for Tarshish to flee from the Lord. Then the Lord sent a great wind on the sea, and such a violent storm arose that the ship threatened to break up" Jonah 1:1-4

What I am saying here is that those who wait upon the Lord like eagles will be visionary. Nothing will happen to them unexpectedly as they see things from a far distance because they have acute foresight and imagination. Again, all those who wait on God in fasting and prayer, expect, look for, and hope in Him will be like the eagle - bigger than anything, powerful in strength to overcome any situation. We will also be powerful in flight soaring higher and be visionary, blessed with a strong sense of discernment and perception.

Another point I want to make clear is that without patience no one can wait; you need to have patience before you can wait. As mentioned earlier many have fallen into big trouble and disasters as result of impatience. Patience is the number one needed tool when it comes to waiting. If you cannot wait, you lose your promise. No matter how you try, no matter how you pray, God has His time and purpose that may differ from yours. It is only through patience that we can see God's glory.

Benefits of waiting patiently: The Psalmist David listed five things which he benefited from as a result of waiting patiently on the Lord (Psalm 40:1-3).

1. He turned to me and heard my cry
2. He lifted me out of the slimy pit,
3. Out of the mud and mire,
4. He set my feet on a rock and gave me a firm place to stand
5. He put a new song in my mouth, a hymn of praise to our God, so, many will see and fear and put their trust in the Lord.

To receive our blessings from the Lord as believers, we need to wait patiently on Him. Hopefully and patiently looking to God everyday is like expecting an important letter or a parcel. Israel needed to wait many years for their burden to be over, yet they were to wait patiently for the Lord. How long have you waited? How long have you prayed? What situation do you find yourself? Patiently wait for Him as He is faithful.

Dangers of impatience: Traffic lights are installed on roads to keep them safe. An impatient driver who fails to comply with the traffic lights faces the danger of hurting or killing himself and others. Before traffic lights were installed in one of the biggest roundabouts in my area in North London on A10 (Great Cambridge Road) in Edmonton, there were a series of accidents. Now that the lights have been installed, there has been a dramatic drop in accidents and the place is much safer. Many people have had a lot of 'life accidents' because they had no patience to wait on God's will. Men and women who failed to wait on God for a right partner have suffered a lot in marriage and others who did not have patience to control their temper also suffer as a result. No matter how fast you begin, patiently enduring to the end is what matters.

Those who patiently learn a trade as an apprentice even though they go through all sorts of hardships will one day become chief apprentices. Appointed by their master, finally qualified and experienced in the trade now almost as expert as the one who trained him and able to train others. Paul said "And not only so, but we glory in tribulations also: knowing that tribulation worketh patience; and patience, experience; and experience, hope: And hope maketh not ashamed; because the love of God is shed abroad in our hearts by the Holy Ghost which is given unto us." Romans 5:3-5 (KJV)

What Paul is saying here is that not only do believers rejoice in the fact that we have peace with God through our Lord Jesus because we are being justified by faith, Christ (Romans 5:1-2) but also in hard times knowing that these periods will produce patience; And the patience will produce experience; and the experience hope. As I said earlier anyone who goes through hardship to be trained in any trade becomes experienced which gives him or her hope of being able to execute anything pertaining to what he or she has learnt. So you see how important it is to be patient in life.

This reminds me of a story of two birds told to me by the elders in Ghana, one of them, in their view, had the best nest, while the other had the worse one, they proceeded to tell me why. The best nests are always built at the tail end of palm trees, nicely with long and curved ends. This makes it difficult for any predator like snakes to enter in to take their eggs or to harm them. The worst nest is flat, open made from twigs and not in a protected place. This makes it easy for the predators as snakes to get to them for their eggs at any time. One day the bird with the poor nest came to one with the good one and asked it to teach him how to make a good nest. The bird with the good nest agreed to do so, unfortunately, after being told that it was painstakingly work to build the foundation, the bird refused to learn furthermore. It claimed it took up too much of its time and that it was going to use its own knowledge to finish the nest. However, it could not and so it ended up with such poor nests that made it vulnerable to rain and the risk of its life. The moral here is never rush, find the time and patience to learn. The Lord has always equipped those who take time to wait upon Him. Those we see in our world today with high qualifications and every experience in positions have to endure patiently in hardships with dedication and hard work. With God's help as child of God you can also do the same.

Right Location

There are so many promises in the Bible about God's intention to bless his children. Those who remain in Him, which means staying connected to Him, individually or collectively as a Church or even as a family. In writing this book 'Staying Connected to Christ', the Lord told me that to stay connected can also mean being in the right location; it has a great connection with the blessings of God. The story of Job shows that during his trouble he was visited by his three friends, Eliphaz the Temanite, Bildad the Shuhite, and Zophar the Naamathite. The main message of their visit was based on the fact that the world is influenced by a system of cause and effect. That means nothing happens without a cause. What these friends were trying to say is a Ghanaian Akan proverb roughly translated in English means "a palm branch never makes noise unless it's been touched by an object." Or "there is no smoke without a fire" they thought Job must have done something wrong to deserve his ordeal as good things happens to good people and bad things happen to bad people. Therefore they believed that Job must be suffering because of some terrible sin he had committed. The three visitors tried to persuade him to repent of his sin. In Job 8:11-13 this is what one of the friends Bildad said, "Can the papyrus grow without a marsh? Can the reeds flourish without water? While it is, yet green and not cut down, it withers before any other plant. So are the paths of all who forget God; and the hope of the hypocrite shall perish" (NKV)

In the scripture above, I reckon that Bildad's basis for analysing Job's situation was wrong, although he may have had his reason to analyze it the way he did. Nevertheless, I still believe there is something positive in his statement; God has created location and places suitable for everything. Fishes live in the sea or in rivers, birds in the air, animals in the bushes or in the forest. Some animals can survive only in tropical areas; fishes can only survive in water. The Lord has placed even the sun and the moon in the correct location. Everything God made was given its pride of place in order that it functions according to His order of things. In the same way, God has the right location for his children a place of blessing. In the context of this subject, I think it is important to learn more about Papyrus. It is a variety of solid-stemmed grass which is native of the Nile region or can ONLY grow by a river or a watery place. It was used as writing material for the ancient Egyptians. A reed is also another tall slender plant with jointed stalks that grows in marshes and other wet areas. These plants can also only grow in a swampy area that is the location and conditions under which God has enabled its growth.

The positive side of this positioning is that God has a right location for everything. There is a right location for his blessings like the examples below.

Examples or the importance of right location

Genesis 12:1-4, "Then the Lord told Abram, "Leave your country, your relatives, and your father's house, and go to the land that I will show you. I will cause you to become the father of great nation. I will bless you and make you famous, and

I will make you blessing to others. I will bless those who bless you and curse those who curse you. So Abram departed as the Lord had instructed him, and Lot went with him. Abram was seventy-five years old when he left Haran." (NLT)

Most times, this quotation has been used when the subject matter has to do with the faith of Abraham and his obedience to God. However, this time I would like to use it in a different context and that is for 'Right Location.' **Genesis 12:1-4** tells us that God wanted to bless Abram but not until he had moved from one location to another. He had to move from his fathers' house and his country to the unknown place where the Lord showed him. You see, location plays a vital part in man's life when it comes to God blessing his children. Therefore knowing the right location of your blessing is very important. No matter how much or less you earn, being in God's purpose or will (right location) is all that matters. Sometimes moving into the right location can be painful, similar to that of Abram's; when he had to leave his country, his relatives, and his father's house. He had to go to the land God showed him. Perhaps it may have been difficult for him as it would have been for anyone who left his or her comfort zone, and be in a place where he did not know anyone. But it was worth leaving; he left and went to, a place where God would bless him. While on the subject of the price to pay for changing location, I am reminded of something that happened when I was in Bible school. One day I asked a teacher a question and greatly regretted after asking it. The teacher at that time was a lady who had been in Ghana for many years as a missionary. I asked her what was the greatest price a missionary could pay leaving his country. To the surprise of the class, this woman broke down into tears before she could utter a word. As a result, she could not answer my question; personally, I believe it all had to do with the hardship she may have gone through in Ghana, in her time as a missionary.

Keeping to the theme of 'the right location', I believe very strongly the reason why most people are struggling all the time is that they are in the wrong location. They are in places not approved by God, and that is like taking a fish out of water and placing it on dry land. It is also similar to placing an animal like a horse to live in a river or the sea; it is most likely to die because it is not the natural territory for it. Sometimes we even move from our right church and our life becomes a mess. People leave their wives and husbands, their matrimonial homes, which is their right location. The result of these people's lives turns sour because they are out of touch with their divine purpose. Others also fail to leave where they have wrongly placed themselves, even though in some cases some realised that they are in wrong place. Many people are in a wrong location because they want to please someone else; others because of greediness and selfishness. Many also refuse to move or go to the place, which is the right location for them because they will be away from their comfort zones.

Elijah was fed by Ravens and the widow of Zarephath in 1 Kings 17:1-9 when he told Ahab the king of Israel that there would be no rain for some years until he had spoken as commanded by God. Since there was no rain, there was also famine, lack of food and water. When God wanted to feed the prophet, He ordered him to go to a specific place. This was to separate himself from the rest of the people who had sinned against the Lord. Elijah was brought to the right place so he could be fed and given drink. "The Lord said to him: "Leave here, turn eastward and hide in the Kerith Ravine, east of the Jordan. You will drink from the brook, and I have ordered the ravens to feed you there" verse 3-4. The Bible says that after the brook dried up the Lord again came to him and asked him to move to another location saying, "Go at once to Zarephath of Sidon and stay there. I have commanded a woman to take care of you."

This means that no matter how hard things become, no matter how bad the economy becomes, God knows His children, and he will see them through. He is well able to locate and provide for you wherever you may be. Back home in Ghana, I have seen many who cried when they received letters of transfer in their jobs. However when they went in faith these individuals described their joy about new places of work God had sent them, and how the new places of work proved to be better than where they had left in tears.

What I am saying here is that if God was able to feed Elijah through ravens, one of the greatest miracles recorded in the Bible, He is also well able to take care of you in the midst of any circumstances. You just have to believe him. God will look after you wherever he asks you to go, even in this time of economic crisis; you only have to stay connected to Him. Location is very important when it comes to the blessings of God. That is the reason why two people could be in the same job earning the same amount of money and benefits, yet one will prosper but the other will not. In the same way, some people can prosper in some countries, but others do not. Then there are those who are moving from church to church, Pastor to Pastor and Prophet to Prophet looking to receive their blessing or miracle. They think that they can do so because of the church, they go to or the type of man or woman they go to see. My dear reader I want you to know that it is not about any of these things; it's about your trust and obedience in the Lord, making sure that you are in the right location in your life. I trust that irrespective of what it takes, you will respond to the Spirit of God to lead your life, to be at the right location in your life.

Right or good people

Another way of being in the right location is to be with the right people - with godly people or fellow believers, - and people with good character. This is also, where the blessings of God can be enjoyed. The Psalmist has a better description when he said, "Blessed is the man who does not walk in the counsel of the wicked or stand in the way of sinners or sit in the seat of mockers. But his delight is in the law of the Lord, and on his law he meditates day and night. He is like a tree planted by streams of water, which yields its fruit in season and whose leaf does not wither. Whatever he does prospers. Not so the wicked! They are like chaff that the wind blows away. Therefore the wicked will not stand in the judgment, or sinners in the assembly of the righteous. For the Lord watches over the way of the righteous, but the way of the wicked will perish." Psalms 1:1-6

In the context of this Psalm, the writer states that being in the right location is when a person keeps himself away from the counsel of the wicked or bad people and does not stand in the way of sinners or sit in the seat of mockers. He said, "He is blessed because that person will enjoy the benefit of the law of the Lord, the word of God by the way of meditating on it day and night." When a person refuses to be in the company of people with bad character and unbelievers but enjoy reading and practicing the word of God, that person will be like a tree planted by streams of water which yields its fruit in season and whose leaf does not wither and whatever he does prospers said the writer. This is when you are in the right location which means being in the company of the right people. Because these people will have good intentions and ambition to achieve better things in life and you will be influenced to do the same. If you want to be like a tree planted by water that bears fruit in its season.

In other words if you want to achieve better things in life and even better life after death, then you need to be in the right location. You must be with the right people, true believers that share your faith and beliefs. Many have fallen from the grace of God and are therefore heading to hell and destruction because of bad company, bad husband or wife and bad friends. For this reason, Paul gave this advice to the Corinthian Church, "Do not be unequally yoked together with unbelievers. For what fellowship has righteousness with lawlessness? And what communion has light with darkness? And what accord has Christ with Belial? Or what part has a believer with an unbeliever?" 2 Corinthians 6:14-15 (NKJV)

He also advised them to separate themselves from those who deny the resurrection of the dead. He said, "Do not be deceived; "Evil Company corrupts good habits," 1 Corinthians 15:33 (NKJV). Good Company will help you to remain in Christ the vine, bad company will destroy your relationship with Him. It will also disconnect you from Him and will result you to become unproductive branch. There are some people who are of the opinion that they can be friends with any type of character even be in a terrible crowd and not be influenced by their actions. I find this a difficult and dangerous thing to do; it is very high risk. I have demonstrated this many times in church where I have asked two people to come forward, stand in front of the congregation and hold each other's hands. I then tell them to engage in a 'tug of war' each time, the stronger of the two pulls the other to their direction. This demonstration points to the fact that if you move with wrong people, unbelievers and people with no ambition in life, it could be detrimental if you fail to pull them to the direction of your good character; they will pull you towards the direction of their bad character. Good association with the right company will help you to stay connected to Jesus Christ while bad company will cause you to disconnect yourself from Him.

Solomon in his wisdom gave this advice. He said, "So you may walk in the way of goodness, And keep to the paths of righteousness." Proverbs 2:20 (NKJV). "He who walks with wise men will be wise, But the companion of fools will be destroyed," Proverbs 13:20 (NKJV).

When Paul wrote to the Galatian church, he advised the believers to be good to each other by helping the weaker ones. However, he also advised them to do so with caution, so that they may not be carried away by their influence. He said, "Brothers, if someone is caught in a sin, you who are spiritual should restore him gently. But watch yourself, or you also may be tempted. Carry each other's burdens, and in this way you will fulfil the law of Christ," Galatians 6:1-2.

Be careful whom you choose as your closest friends. Spend time with people who share the same faith and belief as you and those you want to be like because you and your friends will surely grow to resemble each other no matter your view of this matter. Who is your friend? who do you trust to share your thoughts? Notice that these people can affect your judgments positive or negative. I have always admired Mary's attitude of confiding in Elizabeth her relative, the angel's revelation to her because she believed in her. The full story is found in Luke 1:39.

Also in Acts chapter 12, the Bible says that when Peter was released from prison, he went to where the other believers were meeting to disclose to them what had happened to him. "So, when he had considered this, he came to the house of Mary, the mother of John whose surname was Mark, where many were gathered together praying" Acts 12:12 (NKJV). I totally believe that someone may find it difficult to accept this advice because of someone you may have chosen as a friend or adviser even though that person may not share your faith. Or you consider him/her to be a person with good character but I will still re-enforce my advice irrespective of your view that be careful who you choose as a friend because not all people would like you to be who you want to be.

The Lord told the Israelites emphatically, "come out of them!" that meant total separation from the world for those are of bad influence. The Lord also told them not to follow the crowd to do what is evil or wrong, Exodus 23:2. Many people will do what they do, not because they wanted to do it but because others are doing it. In Bible study classes at my church many young people have asked the following question, "Is it right or wrong to go to night clubs?" Each time the question was answered by their peers who used to frequent nightclubs, they will describe all the activities that went on in these clubs and how these places were unrighteous and filthy. This is something, which only promotes ungodliness, which is against God, they concluded.

Others wanted to know if it is right to follow their workmates to clubs and pubs during the end of year party. Some of the young also wanted to know if they could go to a workmate's or a friend's birthday party. In most cases, refusing to go would bring them criticism and derision. In many cases, some that followed their workmates and friends to these unworthy places to please them found them themselves isolated and uncomfortable throughout the night or the time of their stay. They felt that precious time was wasted for nothing. So in the context of this book, I will say these places are not the right locations for you and as a believer, these are not the places you should be going to, so do not go there and then regret later.

Furthermore, some members and others who are in leadership positions in churches are even a bad influence. So church members must be very careful and stay away from them. I know definitely someone may ask, why am I saying that, but the following scripture proves me right. Apostle John in 3 John 1:9-12 wrote to advice Gauis, his dear friend about the attitude of one of the leaders who was bad influence on other members of the church. On the one hand he spoke very well about another leader who was very good on the other end, he advised him and all members of the church and every believer today not to imitate evil. This meant not to be in company of those who are of bad influence but be with those who are of a good influence and also do what is good. John said, "I wrote to the church, but Diotrephes, who loves to be first, will have nothing to do with us. So if

I come, I will call attention to what he is doing, gossiping maliciously about us. Not satisfied with that, he refuses to welcome the brothers. He also stops those who want to do so and puts them out of the church. Dear friend, do not imitate what is evil but what is good. Anyone who does what is good is from God. Anyone who does what is evil has not seen God. Demetrius is well spoken of by everyone and even by the truth itself. We also speak well of him, and you know that our testimony is true."

I have been in church leadership for many years now and I have witnessed many people in church who have opposed whatever goes on in the church. They are always opposing and criticising the leader/leaders like opposition in parliament. These people are like Diotrephes who in his personal interest loves to be first, fights to become a leader also always wants to be seen and heard. They always object to anything good in the church, the society or the group they belong unless the decision comes from them. Sadly, there are innocent people who may not know the real intention of these people, and fall victim to these individuals. They pollute and corrupt their victims and in most cases some stop coming to church and the others who stay also become a problem for the church as these victims also mostly become an opposition too. Please stay away from such people if you know of any in your church for they will hinder your growth in God. Never say "I will walk with him but will not copy him or will not be corrupted by his bad character," it is unwise to take such a bad risk.

On the other hand, I have also seen as a Pastor and a counsellor, women who refuse to take advice from their husbands to stop being friends with some individuals considered by these husbands as a bad influence because of their bad character and vice versa. In the same way, some children refuse to take advice of their parents not to be in the company of some other people these children are considered as friends. The worse part of the matter is when some of these women and men have giving options to their partners, they will rather prefer to leave the marriage than to let go the relationship with their friend. Others say, "I was friends with her before I married you!" I wonder if these individuals understand the meaning of "And the two shall be one".

Benefit of being with right or good person or persons

The writer of the book of Hebrews also reminded believers of the benefits of being in the company of other believers. He said, "Let us not give up meeting together, as some are in the habit of doing, but let us encourage one another and all the more as you see the Day approaching." Hebrews 10:25. When we meet together with other believers we take encouragement from each other and learn from each other. In my Church people are given time to share their testimony of what the Lord has done for them. This way they can bring so much joy and encouragement that will strengthen the faith of others. It also creates and has a great positive impact. In my previous book "Be Ye Transformed, The Steps to Spiritual Transformation! I quoted two testimonies which I heard from Apostle V O Boafo whose testimony has changed my life and my relationship with God.

In contrast, there are others who stopped doing something good and will not go to church. Their relationship with God became damaged because of what they heard from others. Is your relation with a person helping you to grow in your relationship with Christ or is it damaging it? If this person is undermining your relationship with God, it is crucial that you make the necessary adjustments before is too late. When you have read this book and you are one of those who have backslidden from God because of bad company or find yourself in trouble, you can make u-turn, now! Move away from that person and back to Jesus who is always ready to receive you.

Recently, may be for the first time in many years I decided not to go to church on Sunday because I had not been well for few days. So early that Sunday morning as I lay in my bed I told my wife who was aware of my condition if she could call my Twi service presiding elder. I instructed her to inform him if he could be in charge of the service and deliver the sermon. I had managed the previous night to tell the English service presiding elder of my intention. I expected support and consolation from her but instead she rebuked me in a stern voice and said "No!" She left the room without even looking at my face and instantly I knew I had to go to church even though I was not well. So I rushed down stairs and unto my computer and to my surprise I was directed to a message I had written entitled 'Get Involved', but yet to preach. I went through it and made adjustments as directed by the Holy Spirit.

I came to church fully prepared with my sermon plan to preach in both services. I shared this for God's glory and also to encourage the benefits of being in the company of the right people. May God give you an excellent partner such as my wife, a person who will able to lift you up when you most need it. After the services, the impact, responses and feedback from the congregation showed that the message was one of the best they have heard me preach. Many said how they were blessed by the message, praise God. This to me was down to the good influence of my wife. Many women who themselves did not want to go to church that day would have used it as an opportunity and encouraged me to stay home. She would have benefited by us staying home but the congregation would have missed the effect of the message. If you are friends with or live with someone who is either good or bad, there is a greater chance of copying the person. There is a saying: "Show me your friend and I will tell you your character"

The Holy Spirit promised: In Luke 24:49 and Acts 1:4, Jesus told his disciples not to leave Jerusalem until they have been clothed with power from on high (the Holy Spirit). They needed the power of the Holy Spirit to be able to do the work. He was informing them that this will not happen until they have stayed in Jerusalem. He said, "I am going to send you what my Father has promised; but stay in the city until you receive." What Jesus was saying to His disciples is that they would only receive the power when they remain in the right location, there is a place God has prepared for everyone.

The promised fulfilled: When they obeyed the instruction and were in the right location as they were commanded, Jesus fulfilled his promise as He always does because of His faithfulness. Luke wrote, "When the day of Pentecost came, they were all together in one place. Suddenly a sound like the blowing of a violent wind came from heaven and filled the whole house where they were sitting. They saw what seemed to be tongues of fire that separated and came to rest on each of them. All of them were filled with the Holy Spirit and began to speak in other tongues as the Spirit enabled them." Acts 2:1-4

On the other hand 'right location' can also mean, being in the right country as it was in the case of Abraham; in right job, having right friends, right man or woman or even doing the right academic course. Many people have spent years studying or learning something, but in the end it becomes worthless, and a waste of time, why? because, they studied the wrong subject. Your right location (your place of blessing) can also mean where you can be fed, clothed and get shelter. What do I mean by this? I mean it is unfortunate some people do not mind taking any job or any man/woman or going to any Church. Even though it will damage his or her relationship with the Lord, they will pursue that course of action.

Why do I say some churches are the wrong ones? because there are some churches which have wrong teachings or doctrines. Others have wrong leaders or false teachers leading or teaching them. There are in some churches today whose teachings and preaching are only based on what to receive from God such as how to prosper messages and have totally left out salvation and godliness messages. You need a good church, a church with the right teaching and right leaders who will help you to grow in the Lord. Do not just be moving from church to church because of miracles and fun. Check that you are in the right location, a place where you can preserve your salvation. Your church may be small but it might be the right location where God has placed you; it is a place where your services are needed. It is a place where you will be able to serve God with your gift God has given you. A big church might not be your location, as your services may not be needed no matter what gift you possess. Right location is a place of blessing - a place of peace, a place you can serve God with your gift.

I am a sports fan - to be precise a big football fan and I believe playing for a particular team can also be a right location for a footballer. I have seen some footballers and even some managers that were doing very well in some teams (smaller) but because of may be money and fame left to join other teams (bigger) and that was the end of them and their careers as they failed to excel in their new teams. In most of these cases, some of these players and managers were either dropped or sacked. I have also known people who have left churches to set up their own church or intend to do better elsewhere. However when they got there, they lost all the abilities and chances to use their gifts they had in the previous place. In one of his sermons in our church, Opanin Kwadwo Kyere, a renowned marriage counsellor made a statement and he was right. He said "In most cases when a man or a woman divorces his or her destined wife or husband that man's or woman's life normally becomes wretched and things start to go wrong because the person has lost his or her destined location.

Being in the right location is a place of safety as some places could cost you your life or be a place of death. When you are in a right location, you are safe because God the gardener protects you. When King Herod sought to kill Jesus, God ordered his father Joseph to take Him to Egypt until those who seek his life had died which he did (Matthew 2:13-15). Many people have avoided accidents and a lot of trouble because they listened to the voice of the Holy Spirit. They changed locations such as flights, cars, and trains whilst others moved house. On the other hand, there are those who met their death through accidents and disasters because they were in a wrong location. I have heard about numerous cases when parents have asked their children not to go to places and these children disobeyed the orders and unfortunately, these children met trouble or disaster or even death.

Solomon in his wisdom said that being in the wrong place could be an evil time; you could be caught up in trouble no matter who you are because of the place you are. He said, "I have seen something else under the sun; The race is not to the swift or the battle to the strong, nor does food come to the wise or wealth to the brilliant or favour to the learned; but time and chance happen to them all. Moreover, no man knows when his hour will come: As fish are caught in a cruel net or birds are taken in a snare, so men are trapped by evil times that fall unexpectedly upon them." Ecclesiastes 9:11-12

Therefore, position yourself well; place yourself in the right location and be sheltered under God's protective umbrella to avoid any unexpected trouble. In the context of this part let me say here as I did previously, that when Samson fell in love with Delilah, little did he know that she will betray him to his enemies which resulted in the loss of his strength, capture loss of his sight and eventually his death. The woman he trusted to reveal the secret of his strength, valued money more than the relationship. Judges 16:16-17, records that Delilah, "With such nagging she prodded him day after day until he was sick to death of it. So he told her everything. "No razor has ever been used on my head," he said, "because I have been a Nazarite dedicated to God from my mother's womb. If my head were shaved, my strength would leave me, and I would become as weak as any other man."

To Samson, Delilah was a wrong person, a wrong place and a place of death. Samson's story is a lesson to us all. We must all be careful of who we trust more especially in relationships. There is advice for young people who are reading this book. Listen to your parents' advice and be where they tell you to be especially when the advice is in line with God's word. It could save you from something worse. Do not for one moment think you are wiser or smarter than your parents or any adult who may be giving you advice. They have the benefit of experience added to their knowledge, which surpasses yours. Furthermore, a good parent would not like to lead their children into a disastrous life but a better one. The elders in a Ghanaian proverb would say, "It is not everyone who has been an adult before but all adults have been children before". Note that you have never been where your parents have been. They have gone past where you are now and would not like you to go through wrong paths they themselves may have gone through. I have seen and heard many who have disobeyed their parents' advice and others who have also rejected advice of even church leaders and have entered into relationships, which have turned into a nightmare, and they have regretted but it was late to turn back.

Many young men and women today are rushing for everything in life; they want to get anything they lay their hands on, and quick. Some of these young people want to get married and even have children at a very young age. They do not even care how they get it or where to get it from, all they want is the pleasure these things give. Quite often, these things will lead them to destruction. There are also many who are presumably Christians and who are seeking God's anointing to do His work but in wrong places, others with wrong motives. What do I mean by this? I mean these people are looking in the wrong churches and are with wrong people. If you are going to wait in 'the city' as Jesus told His disciples, this will mean being patient to receive God's power. Some people want to be anointed and doing miracles overnight, they do not have time to wait for God in prayer or time to prepare themselves in the word of God. Others want to be like some men of God who have served God faithfully for years and have been empowered to do his work. What many fail to realise is that patiently waiting on God produces knowledge and experience. This view is wholeheartedly endorsed by Paul who said in Romans 5:3-4 "Not only so, but we also rejoice in our sufferings, because we know that suffering produces perseverance; perseverance, character; and character, hope."

One of the biggest problems between most young people and their parents is parents' refusal to let them go wherever they want to go. Some young people feel because their friends are not under any restriction when it comes to going out, why can they not have the same privilege? Again, I say to my dear young people, especially those living in countries where there is so much freedom for kids and many activities out there for you to indulge in. You must remember what Solomon said. He said we live in a world today that is constantly being corrupted by evil, which has resulted in evil happening everywhere and every day. Therefore be very selective and obedient, take advice as to where you should go. The only guarantee to success in life is to be in the right place at a right time. (Ecclesiastes 9:11)

Some Of Biblical Characters Of Those Who Didn't Stay Connected

Let us consider the results of some people that the Scriptures have recorded, and what happened to them after they moved out of their right location. I believe this could help us as we consider the importance of being in the right location. Paul said, "For everything that was written in the past was written to teach us, so that through endurance and the encouragement of the Scriptures we might have hope." Romans 15:4

Adam and Eve

Adam and his wife had a nice and comfortable place as they were placed in the Garden of Eden (right location). They had everything they needed as God gave them the authority to have dominion over everything except the fruit of good and evil. They had everything that gave them peace and joy, but lost them through disobedience. As a result of their disobedience, God drove them from what was supposed to have been their right location, the place where they could enjoy fellowship with God their maker. That incident was the beginning of the suffering of the human race (Gen 3). Nevertheless; thank God for the second Adam (Jesus Christ) who came to reconcile man to God so that those who believe in him would be put back where they belong - the Garden of Eden, God's original plan for mankind, it is the right location, a place where man (universal) can enjoy peace and joy through fellowship with his maker. Paul states: "For if when we were enemies we were reconciled to God through the death of His Son, much more, having been reconciled, we shall be saved by His life. And not only that, but we also rejoice in God through our Lord Jesus Christ, through whom we have now received the reconciliation." Romans 5:10-11 (NKJV)

Lot

Lot was deceived by his perception, what he saw was a green pasture and good for living. He saw a place of comfort but it was a wrong location. This caused him to mix with bad people in Sodom and Gomorrah where people were committing all sorts of sins which included homosexuality. The result of him being in a wrong location is a lesson for us all to learn. In the context of this book, Lot was controlled by the flesh, what he saw as stated by the Scripture, he chose what he thought was a fertile land. "Lot looked up and saw that the whole plain of the Jordan was well watered, like the garden of the Lord, like the land of Egypt, towards Zoar. (This was before the Lord destroyed Sodom and Gomorrah.) So Lot chose for himself the whole plain of the Jordan and set out towards the east. The two men parted company: Abram lived in the land of Canaan, while Lot lived among the cities of the plain and pitched his tents near Sodom. Now the men of Sodom were wicked and were sinning greatly against the Lord." Genesis 13:6-13 (ANIV)

As you read this book, I advise you to be careful about exercising your judgement based merely on what you see. As we learnt earlier on, our eyes can often deceive us. Be mindful about the results of Lot's choice because of what he saw and acted on, first he was captured in a war and taken captive by Chedorlaomer and had to be rescued by Abraham his uncle as the Bible stated, "The four kings seized all the goods of Sodom and Gomorrah and all their food; then they went away. They also carried off Abram's nephew Lot and his possessions, since he was living in Sodom. One who had escaped came and reported this to Abram the Hebrew. Now Abram was living near the great trees of Mamre the Amorite, a brother of Eshcol and Aner, all of whom were allied with Abram. When Abram heard that his relative had been taken captive, he called out the 318-trained men born in his household and went in pursuit as far as Dan. During the night, Abram divided his men to attack them and he routed them, pursuing them as far as Hobah, north of Damascus. He recovered all the goods and brought back his relative Lot and his possessions, together with the women and the other people." Genesis 14:11-16

Secondly, he was fortunate to be saved from obliteration when God destroyed Sodom and Gomorrah. Genesis 19:12-26

Thirdly, the most dramatic part of this story was when his wife ignored the warning of the angels and so she became a pillar of salt. Genesis 19:17 states, "Flee for your lives! Don't look back, and don't stop anywhere in the plain! Flee to the mountains or you will be swept away!" Verse 26 states: "But Lot's wife looked back, and she became a pillar of salt". Disobedience is a terrible thing, it will disconnect you from God and connect you to wrong people and wrong places. These could attract great punishment and suffering towards you. Therefore, allow God to lead you to choose your location for our own perception may be deceptive or defective. You may be lured by its attractiveness but it could be very dangerous. Solomon said, "There is a way that seems right to a man, but in the end it leads to death," Proverbs 14:12; 16:25. Similar to Adam, Eve and Lot, many people have been caught up in several kinds of problems. They made the mistake of being drawn to the wrong location because of what they have, saw or tasted. "The woman saw that the fruit of the tree was good for food, pleasing to the eye, and desirable for gaining wisdom. She took some and ate it, then gave some to her husband who was with her - he ate it." Genesis 3:6

Do not marry a person because of what you see or hear about him or her unless you see it with your eyes and hear with your ears otherwise you could be deceived. The result may not help you and you could become disconnected from Christ the Vine. Genesis 13:10-11 states, Lot looked up and saw that the whole plain of the Jordan was well watered, like the garden of the LORD, like the land of Egypt, towards Zoar. (This was before the LORD destroyed Sodom and Gomorrah.) So Lot chose for himself the whole plain of the Jordan and set out towards the east. The two men parted company."

Many people do not enter relationships through the conviction of their spirit but by what they have seen or heard. They often ignore the advice of God, which inform their conviction and should have guided their decision. No wonder many relationships do not last that long. As a marriage counselor, I can share this fact through some of the sessions I have had with people intending to marry. In many cases after questioning the couple the answer is often 'I have heard nothing'. Many times, I instantly know that these people have not had the time to enquire of the Lord. Adam knew his wife through his inner conviction so he said, "This is now bone of my bones and flesh of my flesh; she shall be called 'woman', for she was taken out of man." Genesis 2:23. I am grateful to God, as I have told my congregation many times. The very first time I saw my wife I knew in my spirit that she was the one, and would be the mother of my children. It happened this way because of my connection with Christ the Vine. When you have no connection with God, you will not hear when he speaks to you.

As a human being, you may be ashamed of yourself of how you have reacted due to things you saw or head. It might have been bad for you but do not worry about it. It is never too late irrespective of what mistakes you have made in life. Just repent and the grace of God through Jesus Christ the Vine is sufficient to save you. Consider when God saved Adam and Eve and rescued Lot when he destroyed Sodom and Gomorrah.

I take this opportunity to ask you 'What do you think that the right location will be in your life at this stage of reading this book?' Before I conclude this part I want you to have a thorough examination of yourself. Explore whether you are in the right location (your place of blessing). Check your job, marriage, friends and even your church. Is any of the aforementioned damaging your relationship with God? If your answer is yes - you are in a wrong location. You are disconnected from the vine and that is dangerous. My advice is that action has to be taken to address such a situation. Make a U-turn and head towards the right location so there is reconnection to Christ the vine. God blessed Abram when he left his own country. Elijah had to follow God's instructions and went where God wanted to him go before he was fed by ravens and the woman of Zarephath. The Holy Spirit did not come to the apostles until they had stayed in the city (Jerusalem).

Where do you find yourself now? What are doing now? What company do you find yourself in? Are you sure you are in a right location that God can bless you? The most important question of all is: are you saved? In terms of your relationship with God, is your location right? Are you connected to the vine? You must be reminded again as this book nears its end of the 'Right Location' with the key quotation in Job 8:11-13 "Can the papyrus grow without a marsh? Can the reeds flourish without water? While it is yet green and not cut down, it withers before any other plant. So are the paths of all who forget God; and the hope of the hypocrite shall perish" (NKV). If you want to stay connected to Jesus Christ the Vine in order to benefit from His blessings, there is something you must know and understand. To receive the power of staying connected, it is an absolute necessity to always be in a place of His approval. Note that you are not allowed to go everywhere no matter how attractive the place may be. It does not matter whether your friends are going there or not. Some places just may not be a right location for you.

You should also note some jobs might not be right for you no matter how lucrative it may be. They might not be healthy for your growth in the Lord even though it may seem physically attractive. These jobs may keep you from God's blessing. Jesus said, "For what will it profit a man if he gains the whole world, and loses his own soul?" Mark 8:36 (NKJV)

Many men and women today say that their prospective husband or wife must be rich, beautiful, and handsome, have a good status or educational background. Most of you may disagree, but I can say with all fairness that that sort of person may not be a very wise choice as he or she could turn your eyes away from God. The Bible says that when Solomon moved out of his right location and went against God's commandments by marrying women from other nations he lost the blessing of God; those women he married caused him to turn his heart from the Lord. He began to worship other gods - a detestable thing in the eyes of the Lord. 1 Kings 11:2-4 says: "These women were from nations about which the Lord had told the Israelites: "You must not intermarry with them, because they will surely turn your hearts after their gods." Nevertheless, Solomon held fast to them in love. He had seven hundred wives of royal birth and three hundred concubines, and his wives led him astray. As Solomon grew old, his wives turned his heart after other gods, and his heart was not fully devoted to the Lord his God, as the heart of David his father had been."

Many times, we hear about the mistakes that others have made in the past. Quite often, we begin to blame them, we seem to forget that we are not flawless and that we also make mistakes in many ways. More to the point, the consequences of our mistakes could materialise one day. Solomon's experience must be a stern warning to us that men and women can turn their eyes from the Lord. Let Solomon's example be a lesson, which says all of us must be careful. I have seen and heard many men and women who married not because of love or because of approval from the Lord, but because of convenience. They marry the person because of his or her riches or fame and the result of these marriages have been terrible. Someone once said that these people are living in hell on earth; they may have the money, but they have no peace or joy. Many will go to hell because of bad marriages. Someone also said, "One day I was invited to teach in a women's fellowship program themed 'The Effect of Broken Marriage.' We were all very shocked by the contribution of one of the women who attended. She spoke of a Christian woman she knew very well who committed suicide out of frustration and the pressure of a bad marriage". So in the context of that woman's experience I advise that no one would jump into any relationship because of your own perception. Instead you should let God lead you in your decision-making because whatever He gives you is always better without any side effect.

Again, I don't wish to discourage people who seek better prospects in the job market. However, I have also seen and heard about those who have backslidden because of the type of work they got. Of course, I would encourage everyone to get a good job. I would like to make you aware that similar to Abraham, that your job, that man, that woman, that land which has been allocated to you may not be as good, rich or fertile. However, if it is your right location you will surely be blessed. You will prosper and succeed in everything you do for God is able to do whatever he wants to do. In 1 Samuel 14:6 Jonathan states," Nothing can hinder the Lord from saving, whether by many or by few." If God wants to bless you no matter where you are or what you, do or what you have He can still bless you if only your heart is right with him.

Conclusion

Note that when you give your heart to Christ you must live up to the obligations He has set. You cannot re-write the rules of God as you see fit. What people must understand and recognise is that living the life of Christ demands that they continuously bear fruit for His service. You have to do it His way, by His rules, not our own. We can only achieve this by being connected to Christ the Vine and His message, His actions and His ways. We must be guided by His principles at all times. There is power in bearing fruit for Christ, but first you must show commitment, desire, willingness and courage. A tree needs to be pruned, nurtured and watered; to do that the branch of the tree must remain connected to the vine. In this instance, staying connected to Christ is the only way for a Christian to bear good fruit. The point is that if you try another way of connecting - you will fail. You will fail miserably because you are not connected to the right source of power. You need to stay connected to Christ and his word. His words are there to support and guide you to achieving and doing good things. You must be made aware that the word of God is connected to anything that is good. There is only one successful way to do this, "stay connected to the Vine who is Jesus Christ."

God wants to shower you with these blessings and has plenty in store for his children. That is where the joy of bearing plenty fruit comes in. You must use the word of God to fortify the unity of a righteous family, which can assemble battalions of truth to increase your fruitfulness threefold. In doing so your magnetism will produce, a harvest of plenty and your blessings will be bountiful. You will bear little or no fruit without God's will or strength. You can only acquire that strength if you remain connected to Him. Jesus Christ, the Vine is your live link to God, so keep the strings of your heart connected to him if you want to feel and taste the power of his blessings. It is the essence of all that you want to achieve for Christ, yourself or for others.

Conclusion

As part of my concluding words, I would like to say something to my dear young people. In particular, those who are reading this book at this stage. Let me ask you these questions: do you need direction in life or you are confused without knowing which way to go? Are your ways full of darkness, so you make mistakes every step you take? You may be trying so hard to get things right, but the more you try the worse the results become, no happiness in your life and no hope for the future and no security in life. I have good news for the readers of this book. Everything we need in this world to make our lives prosperous and successful is in God's word. Start reading or listening to it, meditating on what you read or listen, and practice it as the word of God and it will change your life. Paul wrote to the Thessalonian church. He said: "For this reason we also thank God without ceasing, because when you received the word of God which you heard from us, you welcomed it not *as* the word of men, but as it is in truth, the word of God, which also effectively works in you who believe." 1 Thessalonians 2:13 (NKJV)

To my fellow adults I say, use God's word to have a happy marriage, a successful and prosperous life, the ability to face life with confidence while aiming for victory. Regardless of how fearful, how impossible things appear or the uncertainties we face in life, God's word has the answers. There are some pressing questions that must be answered: Is your life sour? Are you spiritually hungry? Is nothing going on well with you? There is satisfaction in God's word - Eat it, (meditate on and practice it) as Jeremiah, Ezekiel and David did. You will have the taste of honey in your life; your life will be full of joy, a life with real meaning and purpose. Do you really need satisfaction in life? Not only money or food, the Word is the answer. Jesus emphatically states, "Man shall not live by bread alone but by every word that comes from the mouth of God," Matthew 4:4.

Do you need something that will help you defeat, unsettle and bring confusion to your enemies - spiritual or physical? Do you want something trustworthy that will never fail you? It is the Word - nothing but the Word. Stay connected to Jesus Christ the Vine through God's word and you will be connected to God the Father, the Gardener. You must remain in Christ the Vine to bear good fruit and have eternal life. To make a difference as a believer, be in the right location and you will make your way to prosper and succeed. Just as the Lord commanded Joshua: "Do not let this Book of the Law depart from your mouth; meditate on it day and night, so that you may be careful to do everything written in it. Then you will be prosperous and successful," Joshua 1:8.

Stay Connected to Christ means to remain in Him at all times. This can only be achieved through His Word, fellowship with other believers, through fasting and praying. Another important part of this process also includes focusing and waiting on Him. You will reap the results and benefits with the Power of staying Connected. There is a saying, which brings more clarity to the central theme of this book, which says that, "The chick which is always closer to the mother will always get the bigger share of grasshopper's thigh." Stay connected to Christ the Vine, and you will always be protected by God the Gardener and all your needs will be met.

Where is your dwelling place, in him or outside him? Always remember that 'He who dwells in the secret place of the Most High Shall abide under the shadow of the Almighty', and under God's protective wings. Who do you trust, God or man? Remember that those who put their trust in man are cursed because they are disconnected from God. They are barren or an unproductive branch. However, those who put their trust in God are like a tree planted by the waters, it spreads out its roots by the river because they are connected and as a result produces fruit at all times. There is another interesting point that has to be made – do not try to be clever - by having your eyes on Him and on the things of the world at the same time. Here is another saying which crystallizes this point, "You cannot look through a single hole with both eyes at the same time, you can only do so when you break or condemn one of them". You can perceive the relevance of this saying. When you do this you become double-mind and unstable in Him as James said, **"But when he asks, he must believe and not doubt, because he who doubts is like a wave of the sea, blown and tossed by the wind. That man should not think he will receive anything from the Lord;"** James 1:6-7

Conclusion

This is another serious question for you to consider, "Is Christ in your Crisis?" If your answer is no, please invite or acknowledge Him and He will come in to direct your ways:

- To save you if you are without Christ, that is, if you are not saved or born again
- To help you in difficult times of your finances
- To help you in difficult times of bringing up your children
- To help you in difficult times in your marriage life
- To help you when it is difficult to make decisions
- To help you in a difficult time when you face immigration problems (This is to those who may be leaving outside your native country)
- To help you in a difficult time when people hate you even though you have done them no wrong.

The Psalmist states, "Because he loves me," says the Lord, "I will rescue him; I will protect him, for he acknowledges my name. He will call upon me, and I will answer him; I will be with him in trouble, I will deliver him and honour him," Psalms 91:14-15.

"Because he loves me," says the Lord, I will say in the context of our message "Because his heart is right with me, because of his Godly life, says the Lord I will rescue him". Take courage that so long as you are loyal to Him He will never let you down. Always remember that Christ is well able to do immeasurable things and more than we can ask or imagine. This is possible according to his power that is working within us, Ephesians 3:20. In addition, Luke said, "For nothing is impossible with God." Luke 1:37

Note that in the challenges or crisis that you will face, people will always hate, despise or disappoint you. You should consider Joseph as your guide if you have lost everything and everyone in your life; what matters most is what you have been left with. You should maximize the fact that with God's help you can lay the foundation for greater things. It can change the course of your life, the life of the church, the life of those around you and be a force for good in the world. You will be a shining example of what God want in a believer and one of his branches.

Conclusion

Ultimately I shall remind you of the words the writer of Hebrews: "Let us fix our eyes on Jesus, the author and perfecter of our faith, who for the joy set before him endured the cross, scorning its shame, and sat down at the right hand of the throne of God. Consider him who endured such opposition from sinful men, so that you will not grow weary and lose heart."

Keep your eyes on him and never lose him because if your eyes are on him these are the benefits that are guaranteed:

- Security and provision is always assured
- You will be able to face whatever circumstances you may encounter. There is no challenge life brings that will swallow you up - so long as you focus on Christ. You will always prevail and will always come out on top.
- You will become loyal to him, worshiping and serving Him and in obedience to Him at all times.
- The nature of your confessions will change, and you will begin to speak more positively.
- There will be no room for fear and pride in your life.

- He becomes the center of your life, because you will not do anything without consulting Him.
- There will be hope and faith because you have the word of God.
- And finally those whose eyes are on him are guaranteed to succeed and to prosper: "Do not let this Book of the Law depart from your mouth; meditate on it day and night, so that you may be careful to do everything written in it. Then you will be prosperous and successful."

On the other hand here are also the results of losing Him

- Sinking or drowning in circumstances. You will be overtaken by every challenge you face in life.
- No hope and no faith.
- Disloyalty and disrespect to Him.
- The grip of fear and pride that result in:
- Relying on your finite abilities.
- Depending on the infallibility of others.

- ✦ Blaming people for your failures.
- ✦ Becoming a friend of the Devil and an enemy of the church.

SO:

Stay connected to Christ the Vine and you will have eternal life.

Stay connected to Christ the Vine and you will bear fruit.

Stay connected to Christ through the word of God and you will be successful and prosperous in everything you do.

Stay connected to Christ by focusing on him and you will receive all that He has promised to all those who focus on Him.

Stay connected to Christ by waiting on him and you will be like the eagle growing big, gaining in strength, flying at great height with good sight comprised in visions, dreams or revelation.

Stay connected to Christ by being in the right location and you will receive His blessings.

Stay connected to Christ through your association with right people and your life will be on the right track.

However, if you have disconnected yourself from Christ and are no longer reading, hearing or practicing his word and have taken your eyes off him or if you are no longer waiting on him and you are now associated with wrong people or have become like the prodigal son and have left your father's house (your right location). There is good news for you - it is not too late as the Bible says, "the prodigal son when he came to himself he said, "How many of my father's hired men have food to spare, and here I am starving to death! I will set out and go back to my father and say to him: Father, I have sinned against heaven and against you. I am no longer worthy to be called your son; make me like one of your hired men." Luke 15:17-19. Come back to your heavenly Father and he is happy to receive you back to his kingdom. Unlike many who propose or pray to God and do not back their proposal or prayers with action, the prodigal son came up with his own plan of action and headed towards his father's house. What happened at his arrival symbolises the love of God towards his children. Verse 20-24 says "So he got up and went to his father." But while he was still a long way off, his father saw him and was filled with compassion for him; he ran to his son, threw his arms around him and kissed him. "The son said to him, 'Father, I have sinned against heaven and against you. I am no longer worthy to be called your son.' "But the father said to his servants, 'Quick! Bring the best robe and put it on him. Put a ring on his finger and sandals on his feet. Bring the fattened calf and kill it. Let's have a feast and celebrate. For this son of mine was dead and is alive again; he was lost and is found.' So they began to celebrate. Luke 15:20-24

You may be an unbeliever heading towards hell or you may have begun well as a believer but now you are a backslider or an unproductive branch. You may have wasted days, weeks or probably months before you discovered and read this book "the Power of Staying Connected". It is not an accident it is by divine appointment, God your Father, the Gardener through his Son Jesus Christ the Vine is calling you to come back home. It is your rightful place to enjoy all the blessings that he has bestowed on his children for those who stay connected to him.

Leaving some locations or being out of your comfort zone could be unpleasant. This could mean you have to do away with the following: a woman or a man you love so much; a friend you have known for a long time; your dream job or stop doing something you are accustomed to doing. Note that Abraham had to leave his father's house and his country, Elijah had go all the way to live in a bush by the brook; the disciples had to stay in Jerusalem which perhaps was boring and tiring. The Bible states in Act 2:1-4 that their patience paid dividends; they were empowered as Christ had promised them. "When the Day of Pentecost had fully come, they were all with one accord in one place. And suddenly there came a sound from heaven, as of a rushing mighty wind, and it filled the whole house where they were sitting. Then there appeared to them divided tongues, as of fire, and one sat upon each of them. And they were all filled with the Holy Spirit and began to speak with other tongues, as the Spirit gave them utterance" (NKJV)

Conclusion

The above passage of Scriptures tells us that no matter what our individual agenda or our good intentions are, we must be like the disciples. Our first priority must be to listen to the words of the Master, which is: "stay in the city". God may be sending you as sheep to wolves, but you must have enduring power. Through this book, the Lord wants me to tell you that that place, job, man or woman, habit or character may not be your right location. This also includes even the church you attend which may sound good, nice and be comfortable, but might not be your right location or your place of blessing. You must be willing and obedient to leave and go where He (God) wants you to be. Sadly, some people are in some locations not because they know the Lord wants them to be there, but because someone or something has attracted them to that place. They may also have the perception that the place is nice. Please take note that what is good for someone else may not be good or meant for you. We have individual gifts and talents or differ in destiny as it is said 'The soul of a chicken and a bird is not the same' and another saying, 'No one was present when anyone was bidding goodbye to his God'. I have seen some medicines work for some people but not work for others. Be who you are and stay where God wants you to be.

Always remember that being out of your right location can be dangerous. It is similar to a branch that fails to remain in the Vine and is left out to wither and be thrown into fire to be burnt. As recorded in the book of Job "God created location and places suitable for everything. Fishes in the Sea, Rivers or Water, Birds in the Air, Animals in the Bushes or in the Forest. Some animals can only survive only in tropical areas; fishes can only survive in water. Even so is the Sun and the Moon having their right location given by the Lord in Job 8:11-13 (NKV). In the same way, I believe God has right location (Place of blessing) for his children.

I hope and pray that your hours, days or weeks of reading this piece of information I have offered you will not be in vain. I hope you have been blessed. I also hope it will help you to stay connected to Christ the Vine so that you can receive the benefits or the power of staying connected. May God Richly Bless You!

Other Publications by Pastor David Amoah

Lead Us Not Into Temptation

Be Ye Transformed

Your Future Is In Your Hand

The Power For Your Zero Hour

Guidelines For Preachers and Teachers of God's word

www.ingramcontent.com/pod-product-compliance
Lightning Source LLC
Chambersburg PA
CBHW071217080526
44587CB00013BA/1408